DOGGY ON DECK
Life at Sea with a Salty Dog

Absolutely Everything You Need to Know
Before Cruising with Fido

DOGGY ON DECK
Life at Sea with a Salty Dog

*Absolutely Everything You Need to Know
Before Cruising with Fido*

Jessica H. Stone, Ph.D.
and
Kip McSnip, *The Famous Sailing Dog*

DOGGY on DECK: *Life at Sea with a Salty Dog*
Absolutely Everything You Need to Know Before Cruising with Fido

Printed in the United States of America.

Published by:
Penchant Press International
1752 NW Market Street #310 • Seattle, WA. 98107
penchantpress@gmail.com
www.doggyondeck.com

Library of Congress Cataloging-in-Publication Data

Stone, Jessica H.
Doggy on Deck: Life at Sea with a Salty Dog
Absolutely Everything You Need to Know Before Cruising with Fido/
Jessica H. Stone, Ph.D.
    p. cm.
Includes bibliographical references
ISBN 978-0-9724960-2-5
    1. Boating with dogs 2. Cruising with dogs 3. Sailing with pets
    4. Traveling with pets I. Title
Library of Congress Control Number 20069374488

Cover design / layout by James M. Shipley - Walking Cat Design
Edited by Allison Gross
Photography by Jessica H. Stone*

* additional photographs by Stephanie Hamilton, Neil Rabinowitz and James M. Shipley

Kip McSnip was a salty dog,
And he sailed the seas of the world.
With a keen-eyed captain, a Siamese cat,
And a lovely red-haired girl.

from The Ballad of Kip McSnip
by George O. Allaman, III

Dedicated to
Linda "Bird" Robinson
For feathers and friendship and a
heart as big as the beach.

A GIFT FOR THE ANIMALS

A generous portion of the proceeds from this book are donated to the Northwest Organization for Animal Help (N.O.A.H) in Mt. Vernon, Washington. N.O.A.H. is dedicated to stopping the euthanasia of healthy, adoptable dogs and cats in Northwest Washington by rescuing these homeless pets from partner shelters. They are also committed to "Building a Bond for Life" between pets and their families through quality pet adoptions, dog training, low-income spaying and neutering, humane education, and volunteer programs. Our donation - YOUR donation - from the proceeds of this book is one way that you and I and Kip McSnip can say "Thank You" to our furry friends - those who cruise the seas of the world, and those who play at home.

N.O.A.H. Animal Adoption Center
31300 Brandstrom Road
Stanwood, WA 98292
(I-5 Exit 215)
(360) 629-7055

photo by Neil Rabinowitz

CONTENTS

OFFICIAL HOO HA

SCARY STUFF

PLAY

INTO THE SUNSET

CAPTAIN'S LOG

APPENDIX

INTRODUCTION

Ahoy! Welcome Aboard!

"You simply can't take a long-haired dog to the tropics!" My next door neighbor, Mrs. Glubner, clenched her fists. Standing akimbo she stomped on the wooden porch for emphasis. Kitty P.Q. flew from his railing perch in a fur-spiked tizzy. "It's too hot in the tropics and there are weird bugs in the jungles." She leaned closer. Looking quickly from side to side she whispered, "And besides, they eat dogs down there!" I swallowed hard and glanced down at the fluffy ball of fur at my feet. Unaware he might be served up as a heathen appetizer, Kip McSnip gave me a goofy dog grin and spun his feathery tail in circles. "You either find those animals a good home - here - or go some place safe for your sabbatical." She opened her screen door, paused for a moment, and then shook one finger at me, "Why don't you go to the Midwest? It's safe there. The Midwest is America." Smug and assured, she disappeared into her house.

I spent several nights wide awake thinking about my neighbor's warning. Maybe she was right. Maybe I couldn't travel with a long-haired dog - especially to the tropics. Kip McSnip was my first puppy, and I really didn't know much about dogs. On the other hand, next to my 14-year old Siamese cat, he was my best buddy. We'd gone through a frightening, expensive bout of Parvo together. I watched him graduate from puppy obedience school (with high honors). He'd moved from a bundle of fur-covered silliness to a smart, well-behaved companion. We were bonded - I couldn't give him up. So, what about the cat? True, he was old and a bit of a curmudgeon, but he was *my* curmudgeon. Kip adored his big brother, the cat. Kitty P.Q.

tolerated the puppy. We were family. We had to stay together.

Then I thought about the Midwest. I grew up in a suburb of Detroit, Michigan. It's not safe in the Midwest. I made my decision. I booked a flight, bought travel crates for the critters and packed my bags. Sweltering heat, exotic insects and pet munching natives be dashed – we were going to the Caribbean!

Adopting a puppy is like having a baby; it will change your life in ways you can't even imagine. Kip McSnip, now known as "*The Famous Sailing Dog,*" certainly changed my life. We began traveling when he was just a pup, and we've continued in our excursions for the past sixteen years. We'd never been on a rolling deck when we started, but together we learned to sail. We've cruised the Caribbean, navigated Puget Sound, traversed Canada's waters, sailed the Mexican coastline, wandered the Sea of Cortez and crossed the Pacific Ocean.

Kip went sailboarding in St. Thomas, flew in a float plane over the San Juan Islands and rode a motorcycle in Mexico. He's gone swimming with sea turtles and "herded" wild goats across a tropical island. That old Border Collie has had more adventures than most people. He loves to travel and he's always smiling. In every new port, he spreads love with a wagging tail and a goofy doggy grin.

At each new destination, boaters (and normal people, too) wander over to scratch Kip's ears and to ask me questions about cruising with dogs. Questions like:

- *How do you keep him onboard?*
- *Do dogs get seasick?*
- *Is it expensive to travel with your pet?*
- *How does he go potty on the boat?*

Kip and I wrote this book for anyone who likes dogs, has a dog, wants a dog, is sailing, wants to go sailing and any combination of the above. Whether you're planning an overnight getaway in your powerboat or a circumnavigation in your sloop, this book will help you decide whether to take Fido along or to leave him at home with Grandma. Whether you've got a kennel full of dogs or simply enjoy an occasional tail wag from the neighbor's pooch, you'll have fun reading about Kip McSnip's worldwide adventures. Whether you're doing or dreaming, *Doggy on Deck: Life at Sea With a Salty Dog* will answer all the questions you've ever had about traveling with four-legged buddies.

Using a question and answer format, *Doggy on Deck* is organized into several sections. Each section covers a topic area of concern to boaters who travel, or would like to travel, with their dogs. We use practical suggestions, stories from our own cruising experiences and technical information from the experts to provide answers to the many questions we, and folks like you, have asked over the years.

Kip McSnip and I are pleased to offer our strategies for cruising with furry friends. We've had a blast living these stories, and now, we're delighted to share them with you.

Enjoy and Fair Winds!

Jessica H. Stone, Ph.D. *and*
Kip McSnip, *The Famous Sailing Dog*

THE ADVENTURE BEGINS

How did you get started sailing with your dog?

"Do you want to go yachting on Sunday?" Yachting. Now *that* sounded *la de da*. My new housemate, Debbie Crawsfeld, had graciously invited my furry family and me to rent a room in her home on the island of St. Thomas. She had a dog-friendly landlord and a marginally tolerant cat. The animals got along pretty well; Debbie and I got along famously. As soon as I'd unpacked she started playing tour guide. We went dancing and shopping and met her friends. I'd never been on a tropical island before, and I'd never been on anything larger than a rowboat. Now, Debbie was taking me yachting!

Kip McSnip, my puppy, plus Kitty P.Q., my ancient Siamese cat, and I had arrived in the U.S. Virgin Islands a few days earlier. I'd taken a sabbatical from teaching and planned to spend the year writing the Great American Novel. I dreamed of being a famous author, traveling the world penning my books. What better place to write the first book than paradise? I'd been warned by more than one person that I couldn't take a long-haired dog to the tropics. My friends and co-workers cautioned me to reconsider taking my furballs on the trip. They were concerned about the difficulty of traveling with animals. My vet stressed the importance of keeping Kip and Kitty cool in the dangerously high temperatures of the Caribbean. She searched her data banks for information about foreign strains of disease-spreading insects. One particularly knowledgeable neighbor had even warned about fierce and restless natives who dined on household pets. But these critters were my family, and we stuck together.

While my little buddies watched, I pawed through the clothes

I'd brought from California - mostly shorts and t-shirts, a couple of dresses for clubbing - but nothing, I thought, suitable for *yachting*. I spent an afternoon shopping for white slacks, a tasteful striped top and a smart linen jacket trimmed with gold braid. White deck shoes completed the perfect outfit to wear while joining the ship's captain for cocktails on a private, upper deck.

Debbie said it would probably be okay to take Kip with us but I worried that clumps of loose dog fur would cling to expensive upholstery in the main saloon. I stressed about paw prints marring a polished teak deck. No, Kip would stay home with the two cats. Debbie's next door neighbor agreed to let them all out a couple of times during the day.

Sunday morning I could barely contain my excitement. That is, until we pulled up to the appointed dock. Someone must have made a mistake. The gleaming mega-yacht of my visions had been replaced with a battered, blistered, filthy old boat. A short, old boat. Duct tape, crispy from the tropical sun, held panels of ragged sails together. The back end (it would be a while before I learned the "proper" names for boat parts), was covered with dirty film. Smoke? Grease? I shuttered. It became obvious that no amount of dog fur or paw prints would have harmed this vessel.

"Yo. Girl." A drowsy man with coal black skin and waist long dread-locks leaned over the rails and motioned to Debbie. "Umm-mm, ahoy. Ummmm. Yeah." Soon his equally lucid girlfriend joined him in squinting down at us. One by one, a collection of sunburnt, sleepy-eyed people drifted up from the inside of the boat to the deck. They wore cut-off jeans, halter tops and frayed Hawaiian shirts.

"You're the last ones," a good-looking blond guy smiled at Debbie. "Hop onboard. Now we can go." Because I'd never been on a sailboat and didn't have a clue what to do, I sat quietly in the cockpit, keeping my hands folded on my lap. I felt a bit useless and extremely over-dressed.

We couldn't have asked for a better day to sail from St. Thomas to St. John. Puffy white clouds floated overhead, sunlight drenched the decks, and the little boat, despite its state of disrepair, skimmed effortlessly across the peacock blue water. Cold beers flowed freely, bags of Nacho chips made the rounds and a dozen or more hand-rolled cigarettes passed from hand to hand. Given that I was experiencing the sea - close-up - for the first time, I declined the refreshments and sipped a Diet Coke instead.

About halfway between the two islands we encountered a stretch of choppy water. Captain George, the good-looking fellow who'd greeted us earlier, told us not to worry; this part of the trip was always rough.

"They call this channel Puke Alley," he said. Within ten minutes it was clear why the name had stuck. I don't know if it was the sea conditions or the lunch menu, but everyone except Captain George and me was feeding the fishes.

"Here," Captain George yelled to me, "hold the wheel and look out at the horizon! That way you won't get sick." He left his spot to grab the Rasta man and maneuver him toward the railing. I didn't feel the least bit sick but I stood up and placed my hands on the wheel.

The second my hands touched the helm of that sailboat, I felt waves of electricity roll up my arms to my heart. I knew, in one brilliant jolt, that I was *Home*. For the first time in my life, I knew where I belonged. In that instant, I realized that I am, and probably always have been, a sailor.

It didn't take much convincing to get Captain George to let me pay to fix up his little boat. In exchange for me footing the repair bills, he would take my dog and cat and me on a year long sailing trip down the Caribbean island chain. At the time, I had no idea how much boat work costs but it probably wouldn't have mattered. I'd saved enough for one year away from work. I would have spent every cent I had just to be at sea.

Debbie understood - these things happen in paradise. Captain George was ecstatic. I was filled with overwhelming joy and excitement. Kip and Kitty took it all in stride. Within a week my four-legged buddies and I were wedged securely in the quarter-berth of a 33-foot sloop named *Reve* - that's French for "dream."

And that, my friends, is how *our* dream began.

ABOVE DECKS

How do you get him to stay on the boat?

Captain George jumped to the task of preparing his boat for our down island cruise. From daybreak to cocktail hour I heard him swearing in the engine room, swearing from behind an electrical panel and swearing at boxes of rusty tools.

"It will take about a month to get her ready," he told me. Okay by me - I was happy just being on the boat. Armed with a bottle of bleach and a pair of rubber gloves, I dove into the job of removing years of bachelor grime from *Reve's* interior. Kitty P.Q. adjusted quickly. He spent his days snoozing in the sail locker and his nights patrolling the deck for shipboard mice or little brown cockroaches.

Kip seemed happy getting underfoot. Whatever project we got into, he got into also. He followed his nose through the delightful array of pungent smells aboard the old boat. One afternoon he ambled over to me and pushed his wet nose against my leg. I leaned down to pet him and found a streak of black goo smeared across my knee. Obviously, Captain George was changing the oil.

Dogs and children are blessed to be entertained by simple things. Kip could spend hours on deck working the last slurp of peanut butter from a plastic jar. And, like all dogs, he slept - hours and hours of paw-twitching sleep. I thought about what my father had told me when I first brought Kip home. I'd been extremely concerned about the number of hours the puppy spent snoozing under my desk.

"Don't worry, Red," my father counseled. "He can't color and he doesn't read. He's doing what he does best. Leave the dog alone." Maybe dad was right but still, I worried about him. Was he getting enough exercise? Kip isn't a purebred; he's a mix. He's mostly Border Collie with a little something from down the street mixed in. Even so, he's a herd dog, and they need to run.

Twice a day Captain George and I stopped our work and took Kip ashore for a potty break and a brief run. We were anchored next to a bump of uninhabited land at the far end of the bay. We'd row over to the narrow beach, tie off on a rock, then sit with a cup of coffee or a cold beer and wait. Kip wandered around sniffing things and looking for private potty spots. When he was done he'd scamper back to the dinghy and Captain George would row us home to *Reve*. The hardest part of these exercise breaks was getting Kip on and off the boat. The process was awkward at best, with me trying to hold 45 pounds of wriggling fur while climbing into the dinghy. Captain George would stand in the rubber craft, balancing against the pontoons while reaching up for the dog and me. More than once the three of us landed in a tangled heap in the bottom of the Zodiac®.

One afternoon Captain George and I left Kip and Kitty onboard and took the dinghy to town for provisions. We decided to use the outboard rather than row as we were over a mile from the dinghy dock.

"You stay on the boat," I said, "and guard." I petted Kip's head. "We'll be back pretty soon." Kip stood on deck poking his head between the lifelines, watching forlornly, as we motored across the water.

We tied up next to at least twenty other dinghies. The dock was about a block away from a popular, open-air bar. Local sailors waved and called greetings to Captain George as we walked past with our empty canvas bags.

"Stop in for a beer on your way back, George, Old Boy," the bartender invited, winking. "Introduce us to your new crew!" It sounded like a fine idea to me. A cold beer would be perfect after our long, hot hike carrying heavy bags of groceries. Plus, the bartender was busy skewering bratwurst sausages on rotisserie prongs.

They would be plump and juicy by the time we returned.

Several hours later, Captain George and I trudged back lugging bags bulging with provisions. Stomping dust from our flip-flops we climbed the steps to the bar's wooden deck. Setting my load on a table I saw a flash of apricot fur fly off the deck, round the corner of the building and disappear. I thought for a second... no, couldn't be. But still...

"Excuse me," I leaned over the bar, "I know this is probably silly, but did you notice a dog in here? A yellowish, sort of Collie-looking dog?"

"Oh yeah," the bartender grinned. "He's been here all afternoon. Ate most of my bratwursts, too."

"What?"

"Yeah, he showed up a few hours ago - all wet and kind of confused. But he was so cute, my customers - the regulars - started buying him brats. Friendly little feller - smarter than most of *these* guys." The bartender nodded toward the row of tipsy sailors leaning against the bar. I turned to Captain George.

"Let's go," he said. We gathered our bags and hurried down the steps following the streak of fur. Sweat dribbled down our necks as we clomped across the wooden slats of the dinghy dock.

"Damn." Captain George muttered under his breath when we reached the gaggle of dinghies. Kip McSnip stretched out, fat and happy, on the starboard pontoon of our dink. He gave us a big old doggy grin that seemed to say, "Hi guys. What took you so long?"

That evening we left Kip on deck again and rowed to another boat anchored close by. Over sundowners, our neighboring cruisers told us they'd watched us leaving *Reve* in the afternoon.

"Soon as you guys left, that dog jumped in and started swimming after you," our host explained. "My wife wanted to go rescue him, but the little fellow was doing pretty well, and he seemed to have a definite goal. So, we just let him alone."

As we talked, we watched a group of teens on jet skis circle *Reve*. They were teasing Kip. Barking excitedly he raced from one end of the boat to the other. When he reached the bow he was going too fast to stop. He slid right off the end and went flying through the air, all four paws flailing. He landed in the water with a smacking belly flop. Captain George and I jumped up in alarm and hurried to our dinghy, but before we could climb in, we saw Kip swimming confidently toward *Reve's* stern. Then, much to the complete amazement of our neighbors and ourselves, Kip McSnip climbed right up the boarding ladder. Reaching the deck, he shook a fine spray of saltwater all around, trotted over to a pile of lines, dried off by rolling in them and then pranced to the bow to look for the skiers. And I'd been worried about him getting exercise...

The next day we tried something different. We rowed to the land with Kip swimming behind us. It only took a couple of times for him to learn the route on his own. After that, he took himself for walks. We knew the arrangement would have to change once we got underway but it was a great situation while we stayed put, working on the boat.

Of course, a few of Kip's swimming adventures left us a bit red-faced. Border Collies are smart - too smart sometimes. When a new boat anchored in the bay, Kip would swim over and circle it, whimpering pathetically. Without exception, the kind cruisers would hoist him aboard, dry him off and lovingly feed the poor lost puppy.

Soon after, I'd receive a call on the radio. I'd had Kip's tags engraved with the name of the boat and the channel we monitored.

"We've rescued your dog; he's okay, and we knew you'd be worried."

"Toss him back in," I'd sigh. "He'll swim home." As embarrassing as this was, we did meet a lot of new friends through Kip's little tricks, and his antics got me thinking. Kip made it quite clear that not only did I have a lot to learn about cruising, I had a whole lot to learn about cruising with a dog. Now, 16 years later, I'm still learning - about both subjects. My questions, your questions, and the questions of countless other sailors have outlined the course of study. And, along with a bunch of other tail wagging buddies, Kip McSnip has been the teacher.

How does he get a grip on deck?

Kip was pretty sure-footed topsides while we were in the mellow anchorages of the Leeward Islands. But his experience with the jet-skiers served as a warning. How could I keep him from accidentally going overboard when we were moving? Would he be able to grip the slippery, fiberglass deck when the boat was rolling around in places like Puke Alley? I started working on the issue while living aboard *Reve* and continued to gather information as we sailed with other people. When we finally purchased our own boat several years later, I was ready to make it "doggy safe."

To help Kip maintain traction, I paint a good, non-skid coating on my deck. A high quality non-skid surface does wonders for helping both two and four-legged crew to "get a grip."

Although they've been around since the days of the *Black Pearl*, non-skid deck coats have gone through an evolution. Early versions used ground walnut shells, bits of seashell, and heavy grit sand mixed with paint or varnish. This made for a great grip but woe to the sailor who actually did slip on deck. A scrape against crushed shell could cause serious pain and sometimes infection. The aggressive nature of these products made them better suited for commercial ships (crabbing vessels for example) than for pleasure boats.

For recreational boaters, off-shore cruisers and four-legged sailors, a less aggressive rubberized coating is just as effective as the harsher products and is a lot easier on feet and paws. Today even most working vessels are being treated with more modern types of deck coatings. There are many brands available with most of them offering a wide choice of colors.

There are three major ways to apply non-skid coatings. The first is a "mix in." As the term suggests, you simply mix grains (either small rubber bits or micro-spheres of plastic) directly into a good quality deck paint. Then, just roll or brush it onto your deck. This is my favorite method because I know the wear patterns on my deck, and I can use a little more grit in some places, less in others, if I wish. Some of my dock buddies in the Seattle area use washed sand as an additive to their deck coatings. The advantage of washed sand is that it comes in several grades and is extremely inexpensive. In Seattle, the place to find washed sand is the Salmon Bay Sand and Gravel Company, but it shouldn't be too hard to find a gravel company someplace close to your area. Most gravel companies will sell sand in small quantities if you just ask.

The second method is to paint the deck with a rubberized coating and then sprinkle coarsely ground salt into the paint. You then smooth the surface with a paint roller, gently pushing the granules into the paint. When the coating dries, the surface is washed with fresh water and the salt dissolves leaving a reverse grit pattern. I'm not keen on this method because it's hard enough to keep a deck clean without inviting dust and grime to fill tiny holes all over the surface.

The third, and arguably the easiest, method is to buy premixed non-skid paint and just apply it directly to your clean, dry deck. This will give you an even distribution of the non-skid material. Again,

I prefer the "mix in" method because I like applying more grit to some areas of my deck than to others.

I've listed a couple brand names in <u>Resources</u> to help you get started. The brands I've listed are easy to work with, don't contain poisons (although please don't drink them) and are environmentally friendly. Of course, use common sense in your clean up. Many of the larger, chain chandleries display sample boards showing the results of different non-skid brands. Select the method and product that works best for you. It won't Velcro you to a slippery deck in a storm, but a good quality non-skid deck coating will help to provide non-aggressive, comfortable traction for you and your critters.

How does he "hold on?"

Keeping Kip's nails trimmed also helps him maintain grip and balance when topside. Trimming your dog's nails can be difficult and can actually hurt the animal if not done properly. Cutting too deep can slice into the quick, causing pain, bleeding and possibly infection. Because of the potential risks of nail trimming, many pet owners have groomers or vets take care of this task. However, given the difficulty of finding good vet care when you are cruising long distance (we'll discuss vet care in more detail in a later chapter), it's best to learn to cut your dog's nails before you go. You'll need special clippers - do not use nail clippers designed for people. Most PETCO stores have full grooming services and if you ask, they are happy to show traveling pet owners how to care for their four-legged buddies.

Kip doesn't like "shaking hands" or anything else involving his paws, so I wasn't sure how he would take to having his nails trimmed. But when I took him for my lesson in "Pooch Pedicures," the women in the grooming department at our local PETCO fell in love with ol' McSnip. He spent the entire lesson getting handfuls of doggy treats and copious amounts of free love. He trotted out of that store with freshly clipped nails, a new bandana and a whole new set of groupies. My dog still puts up a fuss when I clip his nails but at least I now know the proper way to proceed and which tasty treats make the best rewards!

Does he ever fall off?

As all boaters know, a man overboard is nothing to take lightly. It's possible to lose sight of a human in fewer than five minutes - even in mellow seas. The same holds true for a pet overboard. Even though Kip wears a doggy Personal Flotation Device (PFD) on deck, I take extra precautions to keep him on the boat. For coastal cruising, pre-cut netting strung between our lifelines works well. This type of netting is available at almost any marine supply company. However, for long crossings I string netting across every possible opening. I purchase extra netting and lash it to the stern and at both boarding gates. On a recent passage across the South Pacific I realized I didn't have enough netting to fill in every gap. This worried me until my crew member, Mike Irvine, came up with the solution. In a previous lifetime, Mike owned a fleet of charter fishing boats off the coast of Scotland. He knows all about repairing fish nets. Using a roll of twine, he "wove" little custom nets over every gap on deck big enough for a squirrel to wriggle through. Mike's handiwork stayed put all the way across the Pacific Ocean. Now there's a crew member with talent!

Because of its rounded shape, the bow area can present a different netting problem. I wanted to net off the curved area around my bow pulpit yet still have access to my roller furling drum and an additional sail bag. After several unsuccessful attempts to get flat netting to stay in place, I purchased an inexpensive, rainbow-colored, mesh hammock on the beach in Tenacatita, Mexico. Its concave shape and stretchy weave made it a perfect fit around my bow pulpit. Yes, it's true, at sea the bow of my sailboat looks like a colorful Rastafarian goalie's net, but Kip McSnip stays onboard.

What are "dog booties?"

Kip McSnip, *the Famous Sailing Dog*, wears collars with nautical themes, the occasional pair of sunglasses, and snorkel gear. He sports a baseball cap now and again. Kip's been seen in a jester costume on Halloween and one year he acquiesced to posing in reindeer antlers

16

for a Christmas photo. But he simply puts his paws down when it comes to booties. He *will not* wear them - on or off the boat.

A couple of years ago I heard about dog booties. They were, I heard, the equivalent of deck shoes for dogs. I thought of all the time I could save by not repainting my deck. I thought of how nice it would be to get out of the job of clipping Kip's nails every month. Yes! Dog booties! The answer to... well... some kind of answer. I started my investigation.

There are three basic reasons for outfitting your pooch with booties. First, if you're a boater, they are designed to help provide traction on slippery decks as well as save your teak finish. Second, they protect a critter's paws on long hikes over rough terrain (or hot sand). Finally, they are used to comfort the limp paws of injured or geriatric dogs. They look like miniature mittens without thumbs. You slip them on your dog's feet then - preferably - Velcro them in place. Some brands require tying them in place; others have a sort of snap and buckle arrangement. By all accounts, the Velcro models are the easiest to use.

Dog booties are constructed of a variety of materials including neoprene, fleece, leather and, for boats, non-marking rubber.

Several designs feature reflective tape on the outside edges of the boots. Prices range from $16 to $60 a pair - you need to purchase two pairs if you want to cover all four paws.

It may take a bit of doing to get your dog used to wearing them and used to walking in them. I've noted a website in <u>Resources</u> that gives instructions on how to help pets adjust to wearing booties. One company, also listed in <u>Resources</u>, offers an instructional video on the process.

The good news: If you put them on your dog every time you go somewhere, they will protect her paws from hot sand, cuts and hazardous materials. Because of the rubber soles, they can provide traction and protect your deck.

The bad news: Imagine yourself, wearing socks -Velcroed to your feet - on deck in the summer. They get soaked with saltwater. They get lost. They mildew and they stink. Or, imagine you're wandering in a remote village on some tropical island. The native people have never seen a dog on a leash, and other than flip flops, they've never worn shoes. Enter you with your pooch. Fido is dressed in a bandana, a decorative collar and matching shoes. Cultural diversity gone wild.

Dogs are amazing creatures - they'll adjust to just about anything we put them through. They'll put up with all kinds of humiliating hoo ha just to be with us. And they do this because they love us, and that's what they do. So, even though a dog must "relearn" to walk each time she slips her booties on, she'll do it if you want her to.

Dog booties don't work for us. They are more trouble, and cost more money, than what they are worth. That doesn't mean they don't have a place. You might want to try making a pair to see how you and your furry friend feel about them before buying a pair (or two).

Our boat has unusually high freeboard: How do we get our dog off the boat?

Today, Kip is a senior citizen. If he were a person, and the seven-to-one year rule-of-thumb is correct, he'd be about 129 years old. As he ages, it gets harder for him to move around (I know the feeling). He doesn't have the agility he once had and can no longer climb the boarding ladder. I've had to find new solutions for getting him on and off the boat. The tricks that work for Kip in his "Golden Years" have helped to solve problems for other boaters as well.

Lifting your four-legged crew member on and off the boat can be problematic if your boat has high freeboard, your dinghy is riding big swells or your vessel is sitting on stilts in a boatyard. There are several fairly simple solutions to these problems.

In marinas, I use boarding steps. If I am living aboard and staying at the dock for long stretches, I make a set of steps out of wood and coat them with waterproof paint. This way I can design the steps to specifically fit my boat. I include a door in the back of the steps for storage. My boarding steps then become a mini dock box.

When I'm living aboard, but moving my boat frequently, I prefer lighter weight, manufactured steps. Most large chandleries, such as Boater's World, West Marine, Fisheries Supply, and Downwind Marine, carry wide selections. Manufactured dock steps are made of molded fiberglass or plastic and can be lifted onto your boat. But they can take up a fair amount of real estate on deck, and they are clunky.

Boarding steps are fine for use in your home port but when you're cruising you'll want a more portable method of getting onto your boat from docks. My favorite solution is a folding ramp designed for geriatric or handicapped dogs. It's also the most portable solution. Most of these ramps weigh less than 20 pounds. They fold to about three feet in length and are approximately 72 inches long when opened. The one I have is strong and supports up to 500 pounds. I can scurry up and down my "gang plank" quickly, and it's easy for Kip to negotiate its gentle slope. Small garden carts (good substitutes for dock carts) and most folding dock carts roll right up the ramp to the deck. Because the ramp is constructed of heavy duty plastic and folds flat, I can stow it on deck, out of the way. When lashed to the stanchions, it makes a great support for fuel cans or other equipment.

Although I don't think it's the best idea, you can construct a folding ramp out of wood. A tip posted by one writer on the on-line forum, Living Aboard Forums - Topic: Big Dog on Board at www.livingaboard.com, suggested covering a plank of wood with carpet for traction. Another contributor suggested nailing slats of wood every foot or so for little grips. Putting a fender under the plank for "water landings" was also suggested. I actually tried these methods and a couple more. For example, I tried sliding Kip down on a plastic float. You know, one of those brightly-colored floats with a puffy little plastic pillow attached and a little plastic stem you blow on until your face turns violet. I imagined Kip quickly and efficiently sliding down the ramp to the dinghy waiting below - a kind of "Emergency Exit" routine like the drawings on safety cards in airplanes demonstrate. Well, it didn't work that way. The float folded under Kip's weight on try number one, landing him in the water in the humiliating position of being the sandwich stuffing between two slices of chartreuse plastic. He animatedly refused to play *that* game again. Another time, a dock buddy of mine scored a section of rubber and steel track from an escalator. He spent a lot of time designing what should have been a fabulous way to recycle escalators. My friend is a sweet guy, and it seemed like a great idea at the time, but trust me on this one - don't even go there. While making your own ramp does work - sort of - the wood can be problematic down the line. Wood swells, gets heavy when wet and splits. It also rots in the tropical sun. Well, to be fair, almost every-thing rots in the tropical sun.

Here's just one more reason for leaving your boarding steps at your home port and purchasing a folding ramp before heading out on a major cruise. A standard rule of provisioning states that everything going on your boat should serve at least two functions. Folding ramps serve at least three, maybe four. One, they make it easy for you to get on and off your boat. Two, they can be lashed on deck providing a solid surface for securing other equipment. Three, if you buy the model that comes with legs, you can turn your ramp into a portable seven-foot long buffet table. And, you can wedge it into your companionway to help an older dog, or a heavier dog, get to deck level. In all honesty, even if you are on a budget and a folding plastic ramp seems extravagant, it will be money well spent.

Boarding steps and folding ramps are great in marinas but won't work at all if you are a live-aboard and your home is temporarily a tree-house. In other words, if you're spending time on stilts in a boatyard. If you plan to do any extended off-shore cruising, you will, at some point, end up in a boatyard. I'll bet a month of bilge cleaning on this. If you've got a huge cruising kitty, well, just stay in a hotel or guest cottage. No worries. But most cruisers watch their budgets carefully and end up camping in their boat during yard time. Your boat will be high in the air on thin stilts. You'll enter and exit your home via a shaky ladder - the more remote the location, the shakier the ladder. Getting your pet up and down that rickety structure can be a scary task. Hey, getting yourself up and down those boatyard ladders can be downright frightening!

When Kip was in his "prime" climbing days, I'd just stay close behind him and hold onto his collar as he worked his way, rung by rung, up the ladders. However, in the past several years, this hasn't been possible. I had to find another way to help him get to the ground and back up again.

A few years ago I cruised with a delightful couple, Doug and Jill Austin. The Austins are experienced sailors. In fact, Doug has written two books on cruising the South Pacific. They are smart, funny and kind people. We sailed my boat from Ensenada to Puerto Vallarta together. We stopped in La Paz for a week to get the bottom painted and to install a new thru hull. It was the first time in over a decade of cruising that Kip wasn't able to make his own way up and down the boatyard ladder. The Austins and I began experimenting.

Our first plan seemed flawless. I'd stuff Kip in a duffel bag, zip it closed and then, using a dock line, lower the bag 15 feet to the ground. Doug would wait at the other end and free Kip. At first, before Kip realized what was happening, things went fairly well. But as soon as I zipped the bag closed he seemed to grook the situation

21

and began twisting, turning and wriggling so much I could barely hold the bag. When Doug unzipped the duffel, Kip leapt out, shook until his fur flew like hay in a windstorm and took off across the boatyard. Our struggles, of course, provided great entertainment for the Mexican yard workers.

We tried the duffel bag method several more times. The yard workers and a group of cruisers got into the act. Kip became increasingly irritated with every attempt we made to stuff him in the bag. He'd wiggle free and go tearing off across the yard before we could get the thing zipped. Soon we'd all be chasing him around the boatyard - under stilted boats, over cans of bottom paint. It was Border Collie rodeo and the cowboys were losing.

Finally, in complete exasperation, Doug - a big strapping guy - just picked Kip up under one arm and carried him up the ladder. Fortunately, I didn't need any more yard work after Doug and Jill left but I knew I'd have to find another way to get my four-legged crew member topside in the future.

Before leaving for our next cruise, I scoured the internet, called vets, spoke with other sailors and shopped every pet store in the Pacific Northwest. Finally, I discovered the Ray Allen Company. This company manufactures equipment used for training and handling working dogs. Military and police dogs as well as rescue dogs are outfitted with equipment from Ray Allen. The company makes a sling designed to lower rescue dogs weighing 50 pounds or more into remote areas. I've tried several other brands of doggy slings, but I like this one best because it's strong and is constructed well. In addition, these slings give protection under Kip's rib cage and belly. If your dog weighs fewer than 50 pounds, you may want to try another brand of sling or use your dog's PFD (most are outfitted with a handle), to raise and lower your pet from the boat.

If you do use a PFD to lift and lower your dog, make sure it provides full protection for his rib cage and belly area. These models are safer and more comfortable for your dog.

As you can tell from Kip's antics in the Caribbean, keeping him on the boat when he wants to get off, and keeping him on the boat when he wants to stay on, are two different issues. When he was younger, the first problem was the toughest. Obviously, telling him to "STAY ON THE BOAT!" was a moot point. Putting Kip on a leash and tying him to the mast didn't work either. He'd wind himself around the stick until he was close to choking. I put him below a few times, leaving the hatches and companionway slats open, but I soon learned that I had to lower the slats or he'd simply climb up the companionway stairs (a trick I thought was impossible) and let himself out.

That dog loved to swim, didn't like staying alone, and wanted to go everywhere with me. My solution? I finally just gave in and took him everywhere. He was going to follow me anyway, so I just let him hitch a ride.

Kip McSnip doesn't climb ladders or hop in and out of dinghies or float planes anymore. These days, he moves slowly and carefully on frail, skinny legs. He stands next to the open car door and waits until I lift him up and place him on the back seat. Sometimes I just carry him up the stairs in the house. He hardly ever "guards" these days. Kip still accompanies me everywhere I go, but he sleeps on the way, he sleeps when we get where we're going, and he sleeps all the way home.

I don't worry about him falling or jumping off the boat anymore. When we go sailing he heads for the aft cabin and, yeah, he goes to sleep. But I don't care if he's guarding or snoozing. I'm just happy to have him along.

How does he go potty onboard?

This is a question we get all the time - sometimes people ask two or three lead-up questions and then hint around at this one. Not to worry, everyone wants to know. There are many different approaches to this issue. What works for us may not be the best solution for you, but we have tried most of them and we'll share our results. Hopefully our experiences will help to shorten the time you and your pet need to spend on this.

At first, Kip simply refused to go potty on the boat. *Reve* was his home, and the deck, his yard. He would hold it all day and overnight if he had to. One time he held it 48 hours causing me to completely freak out. But that was in the Caribbean and the 48-hour passage was our longest off-shore. Most of the islands in the chain (at least in the Leeward Islands) are only a beautiful day's sail from each other so the problem simply faded away.

The problem wasn't a big issue when we began sailing in Puget Sound either. For the most part, we were again only a day away from land at any time. Kip appeared content to simply stop drinking water and to take long naps when we were underway. He seemed to know that as soon as we dropped the hook he would either get a dinghy ride or would be allowed to make a short swim to shore. Although the water is much colder here, and rougher in the winter (we sail year round), it was still relatively easy to get Kip ashore. However, one stormy day in the San Juan Islands, our "go ashore to go potty plan" changed.

I'd taken my friend, Rick, for a week-long cruise through the San Juan Islands off the northern part of Washington State. Rick was new to sailing but he was eager to learn and happy to help with any task that needed attention. This included taking Kip ashore in the dink once we were securely anchored. Our journey consisted of typically mellow Pacific Northwest autumn days and cool, clear evenings. But on the fourth day, ominous black clouds hung low in the sky and the weather reports didn't sound good. High winds and rough seas were on their way. I slipped through a narrow passage to Succia. There are plenty of mooring balls available near this small island, and I felt its protected anchorage would be a good place to wait out the storm. I wasn't the only skipper who'd made that call. The anchorage was almost full when we arrived, but for Kip's sake, we took a few extra minutes looking for a mooring close to shore.

By the time we found our spot, the storm was raging. Under a heavy downpour and against 30-knot winds we tried to secure our boat. Somehow, while backing up to catch a mooring in front of us, I pushed our dinghy against a mooring ball behind us. Rick managed to catch the forward mooring just as we heard a loud popping sound followed by a long WOOSH! The heavy iron ring on the mooring ball behind our boat had punctured one pontoon

25

and our little dinghy had started sinking. I slammed the throttle into neutral then hurried aft to help Rick rescue the dink. Along the way, I slipped and cut my thumb.

For the next ten minutes I bled all over lines, my clothing and the stern rail while Rick and I retrieved the half-inflated dinghy. Luckily the rain was hammering down quickly, washing the blood off my fiberglass deck and into Puget Sound. Most importantly, we were able to harness the eight-horsepower motor before it went under. I wasn't worried about the dink. We were pretty close to the town of Bellingham and I felt sure we could find a place to repair the gash in the pontoon.

We sat inside my enclosed cockpit with "celebratory" beers watching the storm's fury outside. I picked at the bandage on my wounded thumb while Rick excitedly described our adventure for the third time. He had a genuine storm story to share with his buddies back home. As I sat listening to my friend, it occurred to me that I might have a more pressing problem than my torn dinghy: How to get Kip to shore.

The storm obliterated the daylight, and cold water swirled against our hull. I definitely did not want Kip swimming across to land. And I got the feeling Kip wasn't too thrilled about the idea either. In his enthusiastic excitement Rick offered to don a PFD and swim to shore pulling Kip by the leash. I tried to politely let him know he'd lost his mind.

By evening the storm showed no signs of letting up and Kip began to indicate that he was way past due for a potty break. Rick went below to cook dinner while I sat in the cockpit, pondering our predicament. Murky water crashed against the hulls of the boats all around us. Then I heard the mosquito-like buzzing of an outboard motor approaching our boat.

"Ahoy!" A man covered from head to toes in a yellow foul-weather suit waved from his dink. A soaking black Labrador Retriever posed alert and ready in the bow of the small craft. "My wife says you've got a pooch aboard. We saw your dink go down this afternoon. Does your dog need a ride to shore?"

That's the cruising community - helpful, friendly and always looking out for each other. For the next two days, the man with the Labrador, as well as several other boaters (some with dogs, others without), motored over to give Kip shore leave.

As far as Rick was concerned, the trip was a success. We met some new friends, got the dinghy repaired, and he had a cool boating story to share. But the incident with the dinghy got me thinking. Kip was young and healthy and was definitely a good swimmer. But might there come a time when he couldn't go ashore? Would he really need to learn to do his business on the boat? We had plans to cruise down the coast of Baja soon and I expected that we'd be sailing off-shore for several days in a row. This could very well become a problem. I started some serious investigation into the matter.

At first I tried using potty-training sprays and pads. I'd heard they can be effective - especially when training puppies. Kip turned his nose up at them. Then I tried placing a chunk of sod on deck. He wasn't fooled. Following another sailor's suggestion, I brought some of Kip's own feces to the boat. He was clearly disgusted. In complete desperation, I convinced one of my male friends to show my dog how to pee on deck. The plan was for me to go below and the two "guys" to go forward and do their thing. I'd hoped that if Kip observed a trusted buddy going on deck he'd understand it was okay. After a short while my friend came below and reported that although Kip seemed mildly interested, he didn't follow suit.

"Maybe," my friend suggested, "he thinks I'm doing it because I don't know any better. Maybe, if he sees you go, in the same place, he'll think it's appropriate." I wasn't convinced but decided to give it a shot. So, while my friend went below, I dragged Kip to "the spot" and, trying to look as casual as possible, I attempted to show my dog correct boat potty procedure. Kip McSnip was completely appalled and ignored both my friend and me for the rest of that voyage.

I spent hours cruising the world–wide web and chatting with strangers in online pet forums. Everyone had interesting, if not slightly bizarre, ideas. Finally, I consulted a professional dog trainer. He too had lots of suggestions, and I was just about ready to hire him until he told me this story. It seems he was working with a woman who owned a small poodle. The woman and her husband spent a great deal of time on their huge powerboat and she wanted the dog to go potty on deck. The trainer suggested she place a wooden matchstick (not the sulfur end) into the doggy's behind. The idea was that the poodle would try to expel the matchstick thereby starting the potty process. The woman would then praise her dog with lavish love and treats. The dog would associate good things with going to the potty and...yeah, I'm with this, so far. I did have my doubts about Kip holding still for the matchstick, but I was getting desperate.

"Did it work?" I asked. The trainer shook his head. The lady was only able to insert the matchstick a short way into her dog's bottom. Apparantly the wood was too dry, it needed lubrication - something like spit would do. So, without thinking, the woman pulled the stick out of her dog's rear and stuck it ... *eeeeeewwww*. That was it. I drew the line. No professional dog trainer.

I was beside myself. We were leaving in just a few months for the first trip when Kip would not be able to head to shore for several days at a time. I stressed. Would he get some sort of infection? Would he, you know, explode? Finally, one evening in a dockside bar in Ballard, Washington, a crusty old sailor weighed in with his opinion.

"Lady," he said, waving his beer bottle for emphasis, "I 'spec if the dog's gotta go, the dog will go. Leave the dog alone."

It was my last option. I took Kip on a three-day trial sail with no scheduled shore leave. The time was, at least for me, sheer torture. Kip held things for a long time but eventually he seemed to understand the situation and found a private place to call his own. The deed was done! I gave him lots of love, treats, more love and more treats. He seemed quite pleased with himself. It was a great day at sea!

Now (and it's been years), Kip still prefers to find a discreet place on shore, but once he figures out we won't be anchoring for a while, he simply goes to his place and does his thing. Maybe those old-timers really do know what they're talking about.

What do you do with the waste?

Handle dog droppings just as you would any other waste on your vessel. First, obey the Coast Guard's rules and regulations on waste disposal. And of course, follow the rules of common courtesy and good taste. Never throw anything overboard in a marina, a lake, rivers or close proximity to shore. In those cases, simply use your pick-up baggies and contain them until you can dispose of them properly on land. If you are in open water, in an area where disposing of organic matter overboard is lawful and appropriate, you can do several things to make clean-up go fast and easy.

I use the saltwater wash-down hose on my boat to clean the decks. I also carry a collapsible canvas bucket onboard for times when it's just faster than hooking up the hose. A simple method, one that worked like a charm crossing the Pacific, is putting grommets in squares of Astro-turf. The squares fit nicely in Kip's spot, giving him added traction when we're in rolling ocean swells. In addition, with a line through the grommet holes, I am able to simply toss the Astro-turf overboard, let it ride in the waves for a while, and then haul it back on deck. Then we have a clean and sparkling surface, ready for next time.

So, there are lots of different methods for training your pooch to use the poop deck. Some methods work best for young puppies. Some methods are exotic or expensive. I'm not saying that what we did, after trying almost everything else, is the absolute best method, but it was the simplest solution to a difficult dilemma. And, we all learned that old dogs really can learn new tricks.

What's the best way to clean the deck if my dog doesn't use the Astro-turf?

Quick clean-ups are easiest if you have a wash-down pump. Many boats do as it's a great way to get rid of bottom slime and critters hitch-hiking on your chain before it goes into the chain locker. I just hooked a long, inexpensive garden hose to my shorter wash-down hose. It stretches the full length of the boat making clean-ups of all kinds fast and easy. Of course, this and the suggestion below are only appropriate if you're out far enough to dispose of organic matter in the sea.

Another less energy expensive method is the tried and true "swab the deck" system. Simply tie a line to the handle of a folding canvas bucket, pitch it overboard and haul up a pail of sea water. A splash of water, plus a quick scrub with a long-handled deck brush makes for a fast, low-tech clean-up. If your freeboard is low enough, swish the deck brush in the sea and you're done. Don't get grossed out; it's only poop.

RESOURCES

Non-Skid Deck Coatings
Pettit Skidless Compound by Pettit: Silicone oxide grains can be added to any topside paint to produce a rough, textured finish. The Pettit grains tend to produce a rougher surface than other brands.

Interlux® Non-Skid Compound: Similar to Pettit's Compound but produces a slightly less harsh, less abrasive, surface.

Interlux® Interdeck: This is a pre-mixed deck coating that produces a low sheen finish and applies like any other paint. It comes in several basic colors.

Skid-No-More by EverCoat®: This is a combination of acrylic latex and ground rubber. It comes in one color - grey - but can be tinted. You can buy this particular product in fairly small quantities, which might be useful if you have a small project area.

Ultra Tuff Marine Non-Skid Coating: This deck coating comes in 19 colors and can be color matched in batches of five gallons or more (so, if you have a really big boat, you can paint your decks any color). It's water-based, adheres to just about everything and can be rolled on or applied with a spray gun.

Grooming
www.petco.com: Check out their website for a grooming clinic or full-service store in your area.

Netting
www.alnet.com: Alnet provides commercial grade netting to fishing vessels and other large operations. Their products are built to hold under extreme conditions.

www.usnetting.com: This company provides netting in all grades, sizes and colors. This company has the right netting material for any job.

www.fisheriessupply.com: Fisheries Supply Company is just one of the many marine supply outlets offering life-line netting for recreational boaters. Although more expensive than going with commercial grade netting, life-line netting is attractive and is cut specifically to fit most recreational vessels.

www.hammocks.com: If you can't get to a beach in Mexico for a while, take a look at the hammocks offered through The Hammock Company. Their single Mayan Hammock should fit the bow pulpit of a 40-foot sloop (of course, there are a trillion variables here so you'll have to do a bunch of measuring and look carefully at the products before purchasing). The hammocks are going to run about six times what I paid the fellow on the beach (and I'm not even that great at bargaining), but you have to like a company that sports the motto "Accomplish Nothing."

Dog Booties

Furlongs Pet Supply: Sells several different styles of dog boots ranging from ultra-tuff all-terrain boots to high fashion designs in leopard and jaguar prints. If you decide to purchase booties for your dog, check out this site as it has useful information on getting your dog used to wearing them. www.furlongspetsupply.com

Wonder Puppy: This is a useful site if you want to make a pair of booties for your dog. The author of the site gives detailed information with excellent instructional photos. She makes the booties because her very senior dog drags his hind paws (and injures them), when he's tooling around in his wheelchair. By the way, this is a lovely, gentle site focusing on animal rescue. www.wonderpuppy.net

The Dog Boot Company: If you're looking for taller boots (I guess they'd be knee-highs on people), this is the place to shop. The Dog Boot Company makes several models of brightly colored materials. They offer matching bags for boot storage. www.dogbootcompany.com

Senior Pets: This company carries a variety of dog boots for geriatric dogs. In addition, they carry an all-terrain dog shoe specifically engineered for active and arthritic pets. These boots were designed to offer traction on slippery floors (or decks), and for protecting injured paws. www.seniorpetproducts.com

Ramps
Handicapped Pets: I purchased my ramp from this company for just under $200. You can also find ramps at PETCO and PetSmart outlets. www.handicappedpets.com/ramps

Steps
Better Way Products, Inc. (BWP): A large manufacturer of marine storage boxes and steps in the USA. They have been manufacturing fiberglass storage boxes, steps and related products for over 20 years. They offer a deluxe model with a sealed floor and a locking storage compartment. www.dockbox.com

Nautical Outfitters: Offers folding dock steps made of lightweight aluminum. They're handy but are also quite pricey. www.nauticaloutfitters.com

Todd Marine Products: Has been manufacturing marine equipment and marine supplies for over 35 years. Todd Marine products include boat seats, marine supplies, marine accessories, boat equipment and boat supplies. Todd Marine Products operates manufacturing facilities in Rhode Island, Tennessee and Florida. The company headquarters is in Rhode Island, USA. www.toddusa.com

Taylor: Specializes in aftermarket products for the marine market. They offer lightweight, slightly less expensive steps. www.taylor-madegroup.com

Doggy Slings / PFDs
The Ray Allen Company: (for big dogs) www.rayallen.com The best sling available (in my opinion) if your dog weighs at least 50

33

pounds. The K-9 Rescue Sling is made of heavy-duty nylon and 2,000 lb. test nylon webbing. An extra heavy metal ring is stitched on for winch or rope attachments. This sling runs around $160. Visit Ray Allen's website to view a moving K-9 memorial page. They also offer special photo galleries.

Altrec: (for mid-sized dogs) www.altrec.com This company makes a couple of PFDs suitable for mid-sized dogs. The RUFF Wear K-9 Dog Life Jacket (two sizes available) are good alternatives to using a sling. Both of the RUFF Wear jackets offer belly protection. This company also makes a third model - NRS - which is what they call a Master Dog Harness. I don't recommend this particular style for lifting a dog as it uses two nylon straps to secure the vest and does not provide enough protection under the dog's belly. The Ruff Wear Jackets run from about $40 to $70.

PetSmart (for teeny-weenie dogs) www.petsmart.com PetSmart online offers a variety of backpacks, front packs and slings for smaller dogs. These run between $20 and $50 and resemble the packs used to carry infants.

Personal Floatation Devices (PFDs)
PFDs designed specifically for canine sailors are available from: www. rei.com and www.riversports.com

Potty Training Aids
www.101-dog-training-tips.com: This is a thoughtful, well-written online article discussing how to house-break your puppy. If you have a new puppy and you intend to take him/her cruising, you might want to use these methods from the start - on your boat as well as in your home.

Simple Solution Potty Training Aid: This is a spray formula designed to help dogs (best for puppies) learn where to urinate. Other boaters have mentioned that it did help them with a new puppy. I didn't have much luck with it, but then again, Kip was two years old at the time. Available at PETCO and other major pet supply stores.

Nature's Miracle Quick Results Training Pads: We also tried pads similar to these. This particular brand is scented like fresh grass and Pheromones to help remind pups of the outside. They come in several different sizes. This might be an alternative to trying actual strips of sod. Again, these are readily available from almost all major pet supply companies.

You Can Teach Your Dog To Urinate on Command: by Dr. M.L. Smith Seaworthy Publications, Inc. 2003. Before Kip turned one, a full year before we went sailing, I enrolled us both in Puppy School. Mostly, I think it was training for the people more than for the dogs. One of the lessons Kip learned, however, was to urinate on command. When I took him outside and said, "Go potty!" (with authority), he would go - or at least give it his best try. This worked in grassy fields.

It did not work, however, on the boat. Still, the trick was valuable and I'm glad we took the time to learn it. This book describes, basically, what we learned at Puppy School. www.amazon.com

BELOW DECKS

What do you do about dog food "out there?"

Ellen Quinn is an accomplished singer and songwriter. She and her husband are also long time cruisers. Almost all of Ellen's songs describe the joys and hardships of life at sea. One of her tunes (a personal favorite of mine) is called, "Working on My Boat." Using funny lyrics and an upbeat rhythm, the song points out how every job on a boat is harder, more work, and takes more time than the same task done on land. Okay, so, just what does "work" out there entail?

Well, consider provisioning, for example. Everything you need must be purchased, repackaged, and relabeled before you go on a long sea voyage (or even down the coast of Mexico). And if you think provisioning is as easy as a trip to the grocery store, I'm going to guess you haven't really had a chance to do it yet. Not only do you need to pack stuff for your two-legged crew, but you need to remember to take enough food and water and treats for your four-legged buddies as well.

The first step is to select the kind of dog food to take. You might want to take a good look at what your dog is eating now and see if it's the same stuff you want to include in your ship's stores. Now, what does that mean?

All kibble is not alike. Some brands of dog food produce fewer, more compact, stools than others. When you're cleaning the deck (even with the nifty Astro-turf squares I mentioned earlier), smaller stools are better. Just trust me on this. If your dog is currently chowing down on a brand that doesn't produce compact stools, you might want to start switching over to another type of food. My vet suggests doing this slowly, mixing the two brands together a little bit at a time to help the dog get adjusted to the change. She feels that's more comfortable for your dog and easier on his digestive tract than making an abrupt change. This works for us, but you'll probably want to check with your own vet before making any major changes in your pet's routines.

The brands that help reduce the size of stool deposits tend to be premium, more expensive brands. However, I've found that Kip doesn't need to eat as much of them as he does with the less expensive brands. Cost, then, pretty much balances out. Of course, there are other reasons for feeding your pet the top of the line foods – things like nutritional value, flavor, freshness and more. But, on a boat, the first reason I mentioned just might be the one you appreciate the most.

How do you store all that kibble?

Big, wax paper bags of dog food are awkward and hard to manage, even on fairly big boats. I've discovered a trick that works well aboard my boat - not only for dry dog food, but for people food as well. I have several large, plastic Tupperware-type boxes designed for storing blankets and seasonal clothing under beds. There are a couple of places on my boat where these boxes fit nicely and stay out of the way. Each box holds the same quantity as a large bag of dog food. I dump the food out of the original bags so it fits into the boxes and I don't have to get rid of the bags later on. Remember, there are no garbage pick-ups on the water. I put a few dried bay leaves in with the food to discourage bugs. This trick works great for all kinds of dried foods, from flour to rice. Remove the bay leaves before giving the food to your dog. I run a ribbon of duct tape around the lids – just for extra measure – and ta da! Enough dog food for an ocean crossing and maybe a few island visits tossed in.

Buy canned food for your dog the way you buy canned food for the rest of your crew. Figure out how many days, how many meals and how much space you have available.

Once you have the cans onboard, label the top of each can using a waterproof marker, then remove the paper labels. You probably already do this with your own food. It's a good idea for two reasons: First, paper labels disintegrate, which means you won't be able to tell what's in the can. Second, when the paper labels do come off (and they will), they can clog bilge pumps and other vital equipment.

Why not just buy dog food along the way?

Unless you are going to a major tourist area, you may need to purchase kibble one kilo at a time. One village shopkeeper scooped two handfuls of dog food into a worn, several times recycled paper bag and handed it to me. In remote areas, 20 pounds of Purina® might serve an entire community, so don't expect to find economy sized bags. In addition, the bags of dog food that are available have been sitting open for a long time - a great home for unwanted critters. It's just best to have your own supplies onboard.

Do his dishes go sliding around when you tack?

Mildly rough seas or even a tack can send dog dishes sliding. To counter this problem my next-door neighbor, Earl, made a custom table for Kip. The table fits snugly between two settees and holds removable stainless bowls. He cut the bottoms of the table legs at angles so the table stays firmly rooted to one spot. You can buy similar tables from pet supply chains or simply construct one yourself to fit your boat.

Does he go sliding around when you tack?

Kip and I crewed for our friend, Bob, when he moved his boat from Mexico to Canada. Kip adjusted nicely to the new boat with the exception of getting around below. The cabin sole was shiny teak. I was worried that his nails would mar the boat's beautiful flooring. Kip was more concerned with just being able to stand upright without his paws sliding out from under him. We remedied the problem with a simple fix. Bob and I purchased several inexpensive throw rugs in a Mexican market and then cut non-skid backing for each rug. Those rugs stayed firmly in place for the entire trip and Bob liked the secure footing so much he continued using them when he got to his home port.

What if we get fleas on our boat?

You've taken all the precautions. You've treated your pet with Frontline Plus® or Advantage®. You've used flea baths, brushed her regularly, and sprayed her fur with Flea Be Gone® every day. You are a flea-free family. Life is good. Until one particularly lovely evening when a group of like-minded cruisers decide to dinghy over to your boat for a little impromptu sundowner party. They come bearing rum and Cheetos. One couple brings their Cocker Spaniel.

"We can leave him in the dinghy if you want," say your guests as a feeble offer.

"Nonsense, bring him aboard - this is a dog-friendly boat!" Well, you know what happens. Within minutes, your cockpit is crowded with happy, sunburnt friends. Laughter and Jimmy Buffet tunes bounce across the anchorage. Everyone shares a story. The dogs beg for treats and entertain each other on the foredeck.

Two weeks later, you're 300 miles out to sea and covered with flea bites. Your boat is infested; you're too far out to turn around and not close enough to landfall to just wait it out. You have to do something. At home, you'd just grab a bug bomb, seal the windows, set the bomb, and leave for the day. But you can't do that on a little boat at sea. And maybe you wouldn't want all that nasty poison clinging to your settee anyway. So here are a few non-toxic tricks to try.

Diatomaceous earth is a simple, natural powder made from the crushed skeletons of deceased diatoms - a type of either saltwater or freshwater algae. It works on carpeting, upholstery and bedding. It also works well on fur. You can even sweep it into cracks in wooden flooring and let it create havoc for bugs hiding down there. Here's how it works (and the stuff really does work).

"When applied to the animal's fur, Diatomaceous earth scrubs on the hard exoskeletons of fleas. The tiny granules of silicon work in the tiny holes of the flea's respiratory system and in the joints of the fleas. Every time the flea moves or breathes, the silicon grinds away at the exoskeleton, eventually killing the flea through blocking/maiming the respiratory holes or by water loss, as the exoskeleton helps keep in the flea's body water." *from* www.onlynaturalpet.com

The good news about this product is that it is just dirt - well, ground up algae forming a dirt-like powder. No chemicals at all. Although it feels like a soft powder to us and to our pets, it feels like razor wire to fleas and ticks. Its sharp edges do all the disgusting work. The down side of this, if you are on a long voyage, is that you really do need to vacuum your upholstery, carpeting, and any bedding the pets might use. If you have a huge powerboat with a mega-generator and can run a vacuum cleaner regularly, no worries. Or if you have a 12 volt vacuum cleaner and your batteries are topped off, again, no worries. Sometimes though, power at sea is a scarce commodity and vacuuming takes low priority.

If you do have a generator or a 12-volt vacuum and lots of power, you're still stuck with what to do with any living fleas, eggs and other bits you suck up in your vacuum cleaner. Fleas are clever and will get right out of the bag if you don't get rid of it. You may not want to toss it overboard (many 12-volt machines have reusable cloth bags instead of the disposable paper bags used with household machines). Even if you toss the contents overboard, chances are the cloth bag will still harbor tiny eggs or larvae. And double-bagging it in plastic to store it until you land might be a hassle. So, do this: Cut a flea collar in three small sections and drop one section into your bag. Vacuum and then leave the bag tied up tight in a plastic bag for 24 hours. Everything in the bag will die. Take the bit of flea collar out (it will need to be disposed of on land), and toss the rest of the contents.

If you don't have a vacuum onboard you can still sprinkle Diatomaceous earth on every inch of your boat's surface. It may take a couple sessions to get in all their hiding places but eventually all the fleas will die. You'll be living in flea graveyard until you reach a marina and can borrow a vacuum. Still, you won't actually see anything and those nasty bites will heal and disappear.

41

Another natural pesticide is boric acid. It is a safe, inexpensive powder that has a long shelf life and is deadly to almost all insects. If you're cruising in Mexico, you can purchase boric acid in pharmacies. It usually comes in small plastic bags holding a couple tablespoons of the powder. Or, you can buy boric acid in bulk, online, before you head out. See the Resource section for suppliers.

Many household cleaners and pesticides contain at least some boric acid - and in a few cases, like Borax®, boric acid is the main ingredient. Boric acid is mildly corrosive. Although the corrosive effect kills insects, their eggs and larvae, it is harmless to pets and people. Because it's a natural corrosive, insects don't build up a tolerance for it and it doesn't accumulate in human fatty body tissues the way many toxic chemicals do.

Boric acid is used in eye washes, yeast infection meds, suppositories, burn ointments and treatments for athlete's foot. You can mix it with hydrogen peroxide for an effective treatment against mold. And, as many cruisers know, it's easy to make "Roach Hotels" for your boat. Simply mix a little powdered milk with boric acid, add enough water (or bacon fat) to moisten the ingredients then roll it into tiny balls. Place the balls on small "dishes" of aluminum foil and leave them all over your boat when you go away for long periods of time. This is a sure-fire way to kill cockroaches.

To rid your boat of fleas, dust your boat's interior with boric acid (don't inhale it, though). Leave it a few hours and then vacuum. Okay, we're back to the issue of the vacuum cleaner. But the bugs are gone.

Here's one final trick to eliminate your floating home of fleas. This one is a short-term fix that will help you get a good night's sleep or will clear a small area (like your saloon) so you can sit inside comfortably without being eaten alive. You'll have to do a little jury-rigging for this one, but no worries, this is where we boaters excel! Put about an inch of water in a low dish - pie pans work great. Stir in a squirt of liquid dishwashing soap - no need for bubbles. Joy Liquid® works well, but any brand should do the trick. Then rig a light over the pan. You can use a small, 12-volt light or a kerosene lantern or even a flashlight, although I try to conserve my batteries. The fleas will be attracted to the light, make a leap, fall into the pan and, because of the heavy soap, they'll stay there until they drown.

RESOURCES

Tables and rugs
Handy dog dining tables are available in a variety of styles from www.workingdogs.com and www.lacharmedlifegifts.com
Non-skid backing for throw rugs (and anything you don't want moving around onboard) can be found at www.westmarine.com or just about any Wal-Mart, K-Mart or other large retail store. Many large grocery stores now carry non-skid backing as well. Look for it in the contact paper section.

Premium dog food
Premium dog foods produce smaller, more compact stools. Because they are not made with fillers your dog won't need as much to satisfy her hunger. In addition, the odor of urine and feces is reduced once the dog's system adjusts to this type of kibble. Stephanie, the dog food expert at PETCO, spent an entire afternoon educating me on the ingredients and properties of dog foods. She discussed the brands carried by large chain grocery stores, those carried by pet supply stores and specialty brands carried by veterinarians and other health care providers.

The top three brands meeting all the criteria I look for in dog food suitable for off-shore cruising are listed below.

Dick Van Patten's Natural Balance: This brand does not use any fillers (fillers are ingredients like wheat and corn). It comes in several formulas - vegetarian, reduced calorie and three different allergy formulas. The dry food line is comparably priced with other premium foods, however the canned foods are quite pricey - running about $3 per can.

Royal Canin: This is a breed-specific brand with food designed for a wide range of dogs. You can choose food for larger dogs such as Labs, Shepherds and Boxers, or for smaller dogs such as Yorkies and Chihuahuas. I didn't find a blend for Border Collies though.

Solid Gold: This is a holistic blend of natural ingredients. It's the most expensive of the premium foods and can be difficult to find. However, it's made with lamb, bison, beef and salmon. They formulate a blend specifically for seniors and one called Tiny Bits for very small dogs. While Stephanie and I were discussing this brand, a shopper stopped by and became a one woman P.R. campaign for this brand. She told me she was willing to drive 30 miles from her home to a store that carried this brand. Now *that's* brand loyalty.

Flea Control

Boric Acid: Prices range from a couple of dollars for an extremely small packet to $60 for five pounds. Here are two sources to give you an example of quantities and prices.

www.biconet.com: 1 lb. squeeze bottle of powder: $5.   5 lb. tub: $15.

www.alsnetbiz.com: 2 lbs. approx. $16.   5 lbs. $35.

Diatomaceous earth:
www2.yardiac.com: 1.5 lb. bag approx. $8   6 lb. bag: $15.

www.dirtworks.net: Uses the trade name "Fossil Shell Flour™"
                    5 lbs. approx. $14   50 lbs. $45.

FIRST AID FOR FIDO

What if our dog gets sick or hurt while we're cruising?

If you talk with many long term cruisers you'll learn that dental and medical care for travelers abroad is actually quite good, easily attainable and relatively inexpensive. This is not the case when it comes to finding good veterinary care. To illustrate this difference, I'll give a couple of examples of my experiences when seeking medical and veterinary care while cruising.

Several years ago I met a man and his daughter sailing in the Sea of Cortez. The young girl, Patti, was about 13 at the time and suffered from a serious toothache. Todd, her father, asked me to join them while they explored a small village looking for a dentist. After a morning of asking around and a couple of bus rides over dusty roads, we located a dentist. The doctor worked out of a small room in the front of his home. While I drank tea with his wife, the dentist gently worked on Patti's tooth. Todd hitch-hiked back to town to look for a bank as he was sure the dental visit would require a large withdrawal from his cruising kitty. It didn't take long before Patti was up and smiling. The pain from her dental problem was rapidly receding. Because Todd had not yet returned, I asked for the bill. The dentist looked apologetic.

"Ten dollars?" He asked. "Is that too much?" Thanking him profusely, I handed him an American ten-dollar bill. Then his wife gave Patti and me a ride back to town. When Todd finally caught up with us we were happily munching burritos at an outdoor café.

That evening, at the anchorage, we shared our story with other cruisers only to find this was more common than not. The dental care in Mexico is good and the prices are a fraction of the cost for the same work in the U.S. Since that time I've learned that many people - ex-pats and U.S. residents alike - head to Mexico once a year for excellent, affordable dental care.

In French Polynesia, I stabbed my arm with a box cutter while trying to install new carpeting in my boat. I'd been trying to catch up on as many little projects as possible while my boat was docked at one of the island boatyards waiting for engine work. Because of the intense daytime heat, I'd wait until evening to start projects below decks. This project was particularly vexing as the carpet backing was stiff and difficult to trim. Gritting my teeth (and probably swearing a bit as well), I pulled the carpet knife back too far and ended up with the full length of the blade in my left arm. More irritated than hurt, I slapped a bandage on it and continued working. By morning, I had a serious infection and was running an extremely high temperature. I felt woozy and was disorientated. Another cruiser noticed my altered state and called the boatyard office for assistance. The boatyard owner packed me into his pick-up truck and transported me to a local doctor. Although the doctor was closing for the weekend, he stayed to treat me. Even in my state of mild delirium, I was concerned about the costs. Everything in French Polynesia is expensive. I needn't have worried. The doctor was careful and concerned as he cleaned the wound, re-dressed it, gave me a shot and wrote a prescription for antibiotics. The bill, including the medicine, came to a total of $32.

Time and time again I've been pleasantly surprised by the high quality and low costs of medical care around the globe. On the other hand, I've been disappointed by the lack of good veterinary facilities in even highly developed countries.

In the U.S. Virgin Islands, the veterinary clinics were little more than holding tanks - not very well-kept holding tanks at that. Conditions were poor, the cages were small and dirty, and animals were basically left unattended. In addition, costs for even having a pet stay overnight were exorbitant.

By the time I started cruising in Mexico, I'd learned about making a Canine First Aid Kit, but one season I neglected to bring a refill of one of Kip's daily medicines. Rimadyl®, a prescription drug for arthritis, is available from almost any vet in the U.S., but finding this common drug in Mexico is extremely difficult. After much searching, I located a vet who agreed to order some from Mexico City. He'd read about the drug and knew it worked well to ease joint pain in older dogs. When I asked him why Mexican vets didn't carry the drug he shrugged and said, "We don't have very many old dogs in Mexico."

Because it's so difficult to find good veterinary care "out there" I strongly recommend you take some of your cruising preparation time to learn about canine first aid and doggy drugs. Put this on your list of things to do before cruising. It's right up there with learning navigation and figuring out how to fix your water-maker.

There are several steps you can take to help prepare for the illnesses or emergencies your pet might experience underway. Initially, you might want to consult the literature on canine first aid to get a general feel for terms and treatments. Next, meet with your vet to discuss your pet's individual needs. Learn about and purchase the prescription drugs you'll want to have onboard - maybe even take a pet first aid course. I'll go over each of these steps and offer suggestions and resources that will get you started. You'll find that by learning doggy first aid and by assembling his Canine First Aid Kit, you'll increase your skills in the area of first aid for your human crew - a two-for-one learning experience.

What emergency pet care books should we keep onboard?

There are many excellent books dealing with first aid and emergency care for pets. Some focus on behavior, others on medical issues and still others on what to do until you can get your dog to a vet. By using the information in this chapter coupled with material from the books I've suggested below, you will have a fairly extensive understanding of what you need to do to provide the best possible pet care onboard. A small collection of books about your dog's health is an important addition to your ship's library. I've listed a selection of good books on dog first aid in the <u>Resources</u> part of this section.

Should we stay in contact with our vet back home?

Kip gets annual check-ups, takes prescription meds every day (for his arthritis and joint pain) and is current on all of his vaccinations. In addition to our regular vet care routine, Dr. Bonnie Logen (Camano Island Veterinary Clinic) and I meet every couple of years just to go over Kip's Canine First Aid Kit. She helps me keep the kit's prescriptions up-to-date and keeps me informed about new medicines and first aid treatments available for pets. During these visits she usually shakes her head in amazement as I share our latest boating and travel adventures. Even though I've traveled extensively and have spent extended periods of time outside Washington State, Dr. Logen has remained Kip's vet for over a decade. She's familiar with our lifestyle, Kip's needs and the needs I have in caring for him. This close relationship gives her the confidence to write prescriptions necessary for a complete Canine First Aid Kit. She suggests that each pet owner establish a long term relationship with a favorite vet and have regular appointments to go over an individual pet's travel needs.

What kind of drugs should we stock in our Canine First Aid Kit?

For the purposes of this discussion, I'm going to separate software (medicines, both over-the-counter and prescription drugs) from hardware (such as gauze, tweezers cold packs and so forth). This should make things smoother when you meet with your vet to discuss your dog's individual needs. You will probably end up putting all of your Canine First Aid items in one kit but there are some items you won't need to discuss with your vet.

The following suggestions come from our veterinarian, and

from several other healthcare specialists I've interviewed for this chapter. However, these are only suggestions and cannot be taken as specific advice for your pet. Consult your own veterinarian before administering any medicines or first aid to your pet.

First Aid Software:
Prescription drugs and over-the-counter treatments

Eye Medications: Young, healthy dogs love to run on beaches and trails. Sometimes this means getting a poke in the eye. Sticks, twigs and other foreign matter can rapidly cause pain and infection. If this happens, the first step, of course, is to remove the foreign object. You may need to wash the eye before applying an antibiotic. If so, use Opticlear®, a gentle non-toxic eye wash. Next, treat the eye with a triple antibiotic eye ointment. Kip's vet recommends Neobacimyx® - this is an ointment in a tube. It's available by prescription. Squeeze a thin strip of the ointment directly onto the dog's eye. Repeat according to the directions on the package.

Cuts, Scrapes: Neosporin®- This is an antibiotic ointment that can be applied directly to clean wounds. This ointment is readily available in almost any drugstore in the U.S., Canada and Mexico.

Skin Infections: Skin infections include hot spots, red sores on skin, bite wounds and rashes. Use Cephalexin®, an oral medication.

Fleas/Ticks: Advantage®- This liquid medication is generally applied between the dog's shoulder blades (out of licking range). The spot may look oily for a couple of days, but this will dissipate. Keep your dog out of the water for two or three days after applying the monthly treatments.

Fleas/Ticks/Heartworm: Advantix® or Revolution®- Same treatment method as discussed above but this one also works for heartworm.

<u>Arthritis and Joint Pain:</u> Rimadyl® and Glucosamine with Chondroitin. Many older dogs suffer from joint pain, especially in the hind legs. Kip now weighs about 40 pounds. I give him one 75mg caplet of Rimadyl®, two caplets of Glucosamine (1,500 mg) with Chondroitin Sulfate (1,200 mg) and one Pepto Bismol tablet per day. I grind the caplets using a small mortar and pestle and mix it into canned food (which is mixed with a half cup of dry food). Remember, though, Kip is currently 18 1/2 years old. He suffers from stiff joints and has a few other maladies common to senior citizens. This is just what I do for *my* dog. You must consult your own veterinarian before administering medications or first aid to your own pet.

<u>Ear Infections:</u> Zymox® with Cortisone. This is a medicated ear wash. Just squirt, or pour, the liquid in the infected ear. You might want to use an ear syringe for this. Gently rub the medicine into the ear. Go slowly as your dog may be in pain from the infection. Do this in the cockpit as Fido will probably shake and get a bunch of the liquid on you and everything else in sight.

<u>Sedatives (doggy downers):</u> Ace Promazine®- My vet suggests these be used only for extremely stressful situations. She strongly recommends they not be used if the animal is going to be unsupervised. In Dr. Logen's view, dogs should not be medicated on airplanes because they may not know to pant to cool themselves. You should consult your vet regarding sedatives as doses vary according to the age and weight of each animal. Your own vet may prescribe a different type of sedative for your pet. I used to sedate Kip on the 4th of July because he went insane with fear from the fireworks. Now that he's completely deaf, he simply sleeps through any and all noisy festivities.

<u>Pain Medicines:</u> Non-steroidal anti-inflammatories (NSAIDs) such as Rimedyl®, Deramaxx®, and Metacam® are used for joint and muscle pain. For more severe pain, you may need a medicine from the narcotic family such as Tramadol®. Again (and again, and again), check with your own vet or animal health care provider before administering any medications.

Diarrhea: Pepto Bismol®. One tablespoon (liquid) per every 30 pounds. As Kip's senior status increases, so do his runny stools. Adding a single, ground Pepto Bismol® tablet to his food each day has helped tremendously. By the way, I got this idea from my mother. She travels extensively and chews a pink tablet each day she's away from home. After visiting over ninety countries, she has yet to experience Traveler's Revenge. Endosorb®, a veterinary product, does the same thing and is available by prescription.

Keep all medications up to date and don't borrow someone else's meds. Ask your vet to prescribe appropriate doses for your canine crew member.

First Aid Hardware:
Gauze, tape and tools

You'll quickly notice that many of the items belonging in your dog's First Aid Kit are also part of your own onboard First Aid Kit. When I'm re-supplying my Ship's Kit, I buy enough of these overlapping items to go in Kip's bag as well.

- Assortment of gauze pads (look for the non-stick variety)
- Cloth tape (you might want to buy two widths)
- Ace bandage (buy the kind that sticks to itself – no need for pins or other fasteners)
- Rounded safety scissors
- Ear bulb or syringe
- Magnifying glass
- Hydrogen peroxide (to induce vomiting)
- Rubbing alcohol (for cleaning instruments only)
- Tweezers
- Rubber or latex gloves
- Digital rectal thermometer (for dogs, normal temps run between 100.5 to 102.5)
- Space blanket
- Cold packs (be sure to monitor your pet when applying cold

packs – dogs can easily chew these open)
- Super glue – much easier than trying to stitch a wound
- Clippers – to cut fur from around a wound. WAHL™ makes a variety of clippers and grooming tools for pets and people. www.groomingclippers.com
- Duct tape – small roll (hey, you never know)

I strongly suggest you make two copies of your pet's entire medical history and enclose them in separate Ziploc bags or seal them in clear document holders. Some countries insist your dog be vaccinated within six months of entering the country. Even though rabies vaccinations in the U.S. can be good for three years, you may need to have proof of a more current vaccination. Your pet's papers should include copies of each prescription in the medical kit and a brief description of what condition the medication covers. In addition, make copies (proof) of your pet's tattoo or chip information (more on micro-chipping and tattoos later). One copy of these documents belongs in your Canine First Aid Kit, the other in your ship's papers. Most cruisers keep these in the nav station or in the ship's safe. Just make sure they are easy to find should you need them for check-in or for Customs, or to show boarding officers.

What if my dog gets into toxic materials?

The cruising lifestyle is a healthy lifestyle. Did you know that you (and your dog) actually get younger when you live at sea? Still, there are a lot of toxic materials in the world of boating. Just walk past any working boatyard and you can feel your lungs squeezing and your liver wincing. It's not hard to imagine your dog getting into some kind of poisonous liquid or chewing on a chunk of something treated with toxic chemicals. There are a couple of things you can do to help at least minimize the chance of your dog becoming seriously ill, or worse, due to poison.

Probably the most obvious solution is to go through your boat and identify the cans, jars, bottles and bags of toxic materials. Make sure they are securely packaged and store them in closed lockers where cold wet noses aren't allowed. You can manage your own environment fairly easily, but dealing with the boating environment in general is more challenging. Boatyards and marinas are teeming with lethal chemicals. Keep a close watch on your pooch; better still, put him on a leash in potentially dangerous environments.

A less immediate but important method of caring for your pet is to learn about environmental hazards and what you can do if your dog is poisoned. This can be a huge task because there are so many substances (both natural and man-made) that can produce lethal reactions in dogs. To help you with this daunting job, I've collected lists of the most obvious poisons your pet is likely to encounter in the boating environment. I've also suggested an excellent website that offers extensive information about poisons.

The following list of poisonous and lethal household items and plants were compiled by The American Society for the Prevention of Cruelty to Animals (ASPCA).

<u>Foods to Avoid Feeding Your Pet</u>

Alcoholic beverages	Moldy or spoiled foods
Avocado	Onions / Onion powder
Chocolate (all forms)	Raisins and grapes

Coffee (all forms)   Salt
Macadamia nuts   Yeast dough

Outdoor Hazards
Animal toxins - toads, insects, spiders, snakes and scorpions
Blue-green algae in ponds
Citronella candles
Cocoa mulch
Compost piles fertilizers
Outdoor plants and plant bulbs
Swimming pool treatment supplies
Fly baits containing methomyl
Slug and snail baits containing metaldehyde
Antifreeze
Liquid potpourri
Ice melting products
Rat and mouse bait

People Medicine
Common examples of human medications that can be potentially lethal
to pets, even in small doses, include:

Pain killers
Cold medicines
Anti-cancer drugs
Antidepressants
Vitamins / Diet pills

Indoor Hazards
Fabric softener sheets
Mothballs
Post-1982 pennies (due to high concentration of zinc)
Water-based paints
Toilet bowl water
Silica gel
Cat litter

Common Toxic Plants

A
Aloe
Amaryllis
Andromeda Japonica
Asian Lily (Liliaceae)
Asparagus Fern

Australian Nut
Autumn Crocus
Avocado
Azalea

B
Bird of Paradise
American Bittersweet
European Bittersweet

Branching Ivy
Buckeye
Buddhist Pine

C
Caladium
Calla Lily
Castor Bean
Ceriman (Cutleaf Philodendron)
Charming Diffenbachia
Chinaberry Tree
Chinese Evergreen

Christmas Rose
Clematis
Cordatum
Corn (Cornstalk) Plant
Cutleaf Philodendron
Cycads
Cyclamen

D
Daffodil
Day Lily
Devil's Ivy

Dumb Cane
Deadly Nightshade

E
Easter Lily
Elephant Ears

Emerald Feather/Fern
English Ivy

F
Fiddle-Leaf Philodendron
Flamingo Plant
Florida Beauty

Foxglove
Fruit Salad Plant

G

Glacier Ivy
Gladiolas
Glory Lily
Gold Dieffenbachia

Gold Dust Dracaena
Golden Pothos
Green Gold Nephthysis

H

Hahn's self branching English Ivy
Heartleaf Philodendron
Heavenly Bamboo
Holly

Horeshead Philodendron
Hurricane Plant
Hyacinth
Hydrangea

I

Iris

J

Japanese Show Lily
Japanese Yew (aka Yew)

Jerusalem Cherry

K

Kalanchoe

L

Lace Fern
Lacy Tree

Lily of the Valley

M

Macadamia Nut
Madagascar Dragon Tree
Marble Queen
Marijuana
(Mauna Loa) Peace Lily

Mexican Breadfruit
Mistletoe (American)
Morning Glory
Mother-in-Law

N

Narcissus
Needlepoint Ivy

Nephthytis
Nightshade

O

Oleander   Orange Day Lily

Onion

P

Panda   Plumosa Fern

Peace Lily   Precatory Bean

Philodendron Pertusum

Q

Queensland Nut

R

Red Emerald   Rhodedendron

Red Lily   Ribbon Plant

Red-Margined Dracaena   Rubrum Lily

Red Princess

S

Saddle Leaf Philodendron   Stargazer Lily

Sago Palm   Striped Dracaena

Satin Pothos   Sweetheart Ivy

Schefflera   Swiss Cheese Plant

Spotted Dumb Cane

T

Taro Vine   Tree Philodendron

Tiger Lily   Tropic Snow Dumbcane

Tomato Plant   Tulip

V

Variable Dieffenbachia   Variegated Philodendron

W

Warneckei Dracaena   Wood Lily

Y
Yesterday, Today, Tomorrow   Yucca
Yew (aka Japanese Yew)

The ASPCA, founded in 1866 by Henry Bergh, is the largest humane society in the world. Its mission is "to provide effective means for the prevention of cruelty to animals throughout the United States." The ASPCA policy statement reads:

"The ASPCA is guided today by the same belief on which it was founded in 1866, that animals are entitled to kind and respectful treatment at the hands of humans, and that this is not to be left to the compassionate impulses of humans, but is an entitlement that must be protected under the law."

You can find a great deal of information about animal care by visiting their website www.aspca.org.

What should I do if my dog does get poisoned and I can't get to a vet?

The following list of common items and their treatments is reprinted with permission by ChinaRoad: Lowchens of Australia from their website, www.lowchensaustralia.com. When I'm on land, I'm always searching the web and this site is one of the best for everything concerning dogs that I've found.

Acetone
Signs of exposure: Vomiting, diarrhea, depression, weak pulse, shock.
Treatment: Induce vomiting, give baking soda in water orally

Ammonia
Signs of exposure: Vomiting blood, abdominal pain, skin blisters and burns.

Treatment: Wash skin with water and vinegar, give diluted water and vinegar orally or three egg whites.

Antifreeze
Signs of exposure: Vomiting, coma, kidney failure, death.
Treatment: Induce vomiting, administer 1 oz. of vodka orally followed by water (can be repeated).

Bleach
Signs of exposure: Burns on skin and mouth, vomiting.
Treatment: Induce vomiting, give 3 egg whites.

Charcoal Lighter
Signs of exposure: Vomiting, breathing distress, shock, coma or seizures.
Treatment: Induce vomiting, give laxatives.

Chocolate (all varieties)
Signs of exposure: Vomiting, diarrhea, depression, heart arrhythmia, muscle twitching, seizures, coma from high levels of caffeine.
Treatment: Induce vomiting, give laxatives. The lethal dose is 1/3 oz. per pound for dark chocolate, and 1 oz. per pound for milk chocolate.

Deodorants
Signs of exposure: Vomiting.
Treatment: Induce vomiting.

Detergents/Soap
Signs of exposure: Vomiting.
Treatment: Induce vomiting, give three egg whites or milk orally, watch breathing.

Furniture Polish
Signs of exposure: Vomiting, breathing distress, shock, coma or seizures.
Treatment: Induce vomiting, give laxatives.

Gasoline
Signs of exposure: Skin irritation, weakness, dementia, dilated pupils, vomiting, twitching.
Treatment: Induce vomiting, give vegetable oil orally to block absorption, get into fresh air.

Ibuprofen
Signs of exposure: Vomiting, stomach ulceration, kidney failure.
Treatment: Induce vomiting, give laxatives, may need IV fluids.

Kerosene/Fuel Oil
Signs of exposure: Vomiting, breathing distress, shock, coma or seizures.
Treatment: Induce vomiting, give laxatives, give vegetable oil orally to block absorption.

Lead
Signs of exposure: Vomiting, diarrhea, anemia, neurological symptoms, blindness, seizures, coma.
Treatment: Induce vomiting, give laxatives, remove source of lead.

Lime
Signs of exposure: Skin irritant, burns.
Treatment: Wash skin with copious soap and water.

Lye
Signs of exposure: Vomiting blood, abdominal pain, skin blisters and burns.
Treatment: Wash skin with water and vinegar, give diluted water and vinegar orally or three egg whites.

Organophosphate Insecticides
Signs of exposure: Excess drooling, weakness, seizures, vomiting, dilated pupils.
Treatment: Wash off insecticide, administer atropine sulphate as antidote.

Paint Thinner
Signs of exposure: Vomiting, breathing distress, shock, coma or seizures.
Treatment: Induce vomiting, give laxatives.

Phenol Cleaners
Signs of exposure: Nausea, vomiting, shock, liver or kidney failure.
Treatment: Wash off skin, induce vomiting, give 3 egg whites or milk orally.

Rat Poison
Signs of exposure: Excess bleeding, anemia, cyanosis.
Treatment: Induce vomiting, requires vitamin K injections.

Rubbing Alcohol
Signs of exposure: Weakness, lack of coordination, blindness, coma, dilated pupils, vomiting and diarrhea.
Treatment: Induce vomiting, give baking soda in water to neutralize acidosis.

Strychnine
Signs of exposure: Dilated pupils, respiratory distress, rigid muscles, seizures and spasms with loud noises or stimulus, brown urine.
Treatment: Induce vomiting, keep dog in a dark quiet place.

Turpentine
Signs of exposure: Vomiting, diarrhea, bloody urine, neurological disorientation, coma, breathing distress.
Treatment: Induce vomiting, give vegetable oil by mouth to block absorption, give laxatives.

Tylenol
Signs of exposure: Depression, fast heart rate, brown urine, anemia.
Treatment: Induce vomiting; give 500 mg vitamin C per 25 pounds, followed by baking soda in water.

How do I induce vomiting in my dog?

A common treatment for poisoning is to induce vomiting. There are a couple of simple ways to do this (for your dog). Administer one teaspoon of Ipecac syrup (for small to medium sized dogs - one tablespoon for large dogs). Encourage your pet to drink water following the Ipecac. If you don't have Ipecac aboard you can use hydrogen peroxide to induce vomiting. Give smaller dogs one tablespoon and larger pets up to three tablespoons orally. Then wait. If your pet hasn't vomited within 20 minutes, repeat the process but cut the dose in half. My vet stresses that vomiting should only be induced within 30 minutes to two hours of exposure. *After two hours do not induce vomiting.*

How do I give my dog a laxative?

Use one teaspoon of mineral oil for small dogs (under 30 lbs.), a tablespoon for medium sized dogs, (30 - 50 lbs.) and two tablespoons for larger dogs. You can mix this with food if he'll eat, or slowly drip it into this throat with a turkey baster.

Are human treatments bad for dogs?

Sometimes. Never give your dog Tylenol® or any product containing ibuprofen (such as Nuprin®, Advil®, Motrin®, Aleve®, etc.). These products are toxic to the liver and can be fatal to dogs - even in small amounts. Avoid treating dogs with any product containing zinc (many burn ointments contain zinc), as it can cause serious stomach irritation. Avoid treating your dog's psychological issues with chocolate. I've learned that a cup of hot chocolate or a bar of good dark chocolate is a rare and unexpected treat at sea and can work wonders with irritable or antsy crew members - but that's only for my two-legged crew members. Chocolate causes vomiting, diarrhea, muscle twitching, seizures and a bunch of other nasty symptoms in dogs. If your dog does get into your "people stash," induce vomiting and/or give a strong laxative. And please don't treat your dog with any mosquito spray intended for humans. Many of them contain DEET – a chemical dump in every squirt.

Our dog keeps gnawing at her bandages: What should we do?

A vet would sell you an expensive collar, sometimes called an "Elizabethan Collar." But you can make a device yourself to keep your dog from reaching her wounds while she heals. If you have a small dog, cut a hole in a stiff paper plate. Cut a slit from the edge of the plate to the hole in the center. Slip the collar round your dog's neck and use duct tape to fasten the edges of the cut together.

For larger dogs, try cutting a hole in the bottom of a plastic bucket. If you can't bear to part with your bucket, then sacrifice one of your large Tupperware type boxes. Cut plastic can be dangerously sharp around your dog's neck so be sure to file the edges of the neck hole or melt them with a lighter. It would be really easy if you had a big, lightweight lampshade onboard, but... nah, probably not.

RESOURCES

Books and DVDs

First Aid for the Active Dog by Sid Gustafson, DVM. Published by Alpine Publications, 2003. $14.95 www.cleanrun.com
Kip's vet recommended this book to us. It offers first aid treatment for emergencies dogs might encounter outdoors during work or play. It also explains how to "evaluate the seriousness of your dog's illness or injury." It's lightweight and easy to toss in a Ditch Bag if necessary.

Small Animal Toxicology by Michael E. Peterson, DVM and Patricia A Talcott, Ph.D. Published by W.B. Saunders Co., 2006 $78.95 www. uselsevierhealth.com
This book was written for professional animal health-care workers and veterinarians. It's thick, uses small print and like many medical books, it's packed with complicated technical information. On the other hand, it offers a world of information about lethal and potentially lethal substances your dog might encounter while traveling. While complex, it is a valuable resource. It's rather pricey so you might want to check it out (or just review it) at your local library to see if you'd benefit from having it aboard. You may wish to make copies of useful sections.

Dog First Aid: Emergency Care for the Hunting, Working and Outdoor Dog – A Field Guide by Randy Acker, DVM and Jim Fergus, 1999, Wilderness Adventures Press, Belgrade, MT. $11.95 www.amazon.com
By its nature as a field guide, Dog First Aid is concise, clearly written and easy to tote around. It covers a wide scope of topics such as poisons, vomiting, fractures, burns, fish hooks, injuries and heat stroke. At sea, and traveling in remote areas, vets are not available, so some of the suggestions regarding stabilizing the animal before reaching a vet are not as helpful as sailors might like. On the flip side, this handy little book is nicely organized and veterinary advice will be easy to access in the case of an emergency.

<u>Pet First Aid</u> by Bobbie Mammato, DVM, MPH. Published by the American Red Cross $12.95 <u>www.redcross.org/store</u>
The focus of this 111-page book is on assisting your pet in a disaster. It includes useful information on performing CPR and how to determine if an incident really is an emergency. The American Red Cross offers a series of short, concise books designed to assist people in all sorts of emergencies and disasters.

<u>Emergency First Aid</u> DVD by the Ray Allen Company <u>www.rayallen.com</u>
A 50-minute course in pet CPR, how to recognize and treat shock, what to do in case of poisoning and more. This is used to help train professional handlers who work with police, military and rescue dogs.

THE NATURALLY HAPPY, HEALTHY HOUND

*We don't like using chemicals or pharmaceuticals
on our pet. Are there more natural products we can
take in our dog's onboard medical kit?*

Yes, absolutely. More and more cruisers are asking about natural
health care for their pets. Personally, I subscribe to a blending of
two divergent schools of thought: "Mr. Natural" and "Better Living
Through Chemistry." I figure, take what works and leave the rest
in peace.

Some prescription meds and chemical treatments work well
for Kip and me, and at the same time, we both rely on holistic treatments - products made from essential oils and old fashioned "home
remedies." I'll offer what works for me and what works for some
of our boating friends who travel with their pets. And, as I've done
throughout this book, I'll suggest some excellent websites relating to
the subject. The rest is up to you, your vet or health care provider,
and of course, your best four-legged buddy.

*What should we do about the
creepy, crawly, biting buggers?*

I won't leave the dock without a product called Flea Be Gone®
by Here, There and Beyond (HTB). HTB is a small company based
in Washington State. They carry a small, carefully monitored line of
products. All of the products in the line are blends of essential oils
and because essential oils are natural preservatives, the products have
an extremely long shelf life. They also smell great. Flea Be Gone® is

a formula of therapeutic quality essential oils designed to chase fleas, ticks & mites from your four-legged friends. Its formula includes citronella, lemongrass, eucalyptus and cedar wood and is intended only for external use. Flea Be Gone® comes in two applications, a concentrate and a spray.

Although I have only used the spray on Kip, the company strongly recommends that for best results, consumers use the concentrate and spray together. The concentrate is applied by putting a few drops in the palm of your hand and rubbing it into Fido's paws in both the morning and at night. The reason I don't use the concentrate with Kip is that he has a fit when anyone tries to touch his paws. Trimming his nails every month is a real circus; that's enough paw holding for us!

But the spray is another story. Kip is quite content to sit still while I treat his fur with the spray version of Flea Be Gone®.

Shake the can and then spray Flea Be Gone® on your dog's back, shoulders, legs and belly. You can use the spray as many times a day as you wish (you definitely need to reapply after a swim). You can also spray his bedding and any area where he spends a lot of time. If you're going to take your dog for a walk in an area potentially crawling with ticks, be sure to spray him before and after your walk.

Kip managed to get a nasty case of ticks in Mexico. The horrid little buggers had babies and it took several intense, medicated baths, sprays, chemical applications and a whole bunch of "hand-picking" to rid him of these awful creatures. If I'd been more vigilant in using this spray with Kip, we both could have avoided a bout with the creepy crawlies.

Another great use for the spray application of Flea Be Gone® is in and around your own bunk. In the Marquesas and the Tuamotoes I learned that spraying my pillowcase (and even my hair) before bed kept mosquitoes outside an invisible net. I could hear them buzzing around the aft cabin but they left me alone. The product is all natural so I feel comfortable having it on my pillowcase. There's no way I'd put my head on a deet-soaked pillow! I've tried burning coils or citronella oil lamps in my cabin but end up getting a terrific headache (not to mention I'm a bit shy about falling asleep onboard with anything burning). Flea Be Gone® is a great alternative for both Kip and for me.

Garlic is a time-honored treatment for many ailments. People all over the world take garlic as a way of warding off illness. Both traditional and alternative medicine hold that garlic can help to lower cholesterol and can prevent blood clots. People suffering with rheumatoid arthritis sometimes find garlic useful in reducing pain and swelling. As a natural antioxidant, garlic helps promote friendly bacteria in the digestive tract. This common herb has been used for centuries as an effective antibiotic because it kills some bacteria, fungi and, yes, parasites. Many holistic veterinarians recommend giving garlic tablets to dogs as a means of pest control. I haven't tried taking garlic tablets or giving them to Kip, but several of my dock buddies in cold, wet, windy Ballard, Washington swear by it as a winter-time cure-all.

We discussed Diatomaceaus earth earlier. Again, it is a simple powder made from the crushed skeletons of deceased saltwater or fresh water algae. It's non-toxic and odorless. I've tried this with both Kip and my Siamese cat, Kitty P.Q. This stuff really works.

Are there natural remedies for cuts, bumps and bruises?

As I mentioned in the section on assembling a First Aid Kit for Fido, many of the items - both medicines and instruments - used for human care are also employed in veterinary medicine. This is true for holistic vet care as well.

Arnica Montana (Leopard's Bane) is a holistic treatment that works well on people as well as their pets. I learned about this when I slammed a forward hatch cover on my right foot. Apparently my vocal response to the incident was loud (and specific) enough for my neighbor, two boats away, to hear. She's a naturopath and midwife and as soon as she figured out the cause of my distress, she came running down the dock with a tube of cream and a plastic vial of tiny, white tablets.

"Here," she said, thrusting the tube at me, "rub this cream into your foot; get it on there fast." I took the tube. I was in too much agony to argue. Then she poured four or five of the little tablets into the cap of the plastic tube and told me to let them dissolve under my tongue. Well, I have to be honest, I've suffered a bunch of "boat bites" over the years and I know that bruises get ugly. Then they get really, really ugly; then they get sort of disgusting, and then they go away. But this bruise, the one that should have been a whopper, barely developed at all! And the pain was significantly less than what I expected. Needless to say, I was interested in this stuff.

My neighbor explained that the sooner you apply Arnica to a bruise or injured muscle, the better it works. It's extremely effective not only for use on bruises but for any muscle soreness, and even arthritis pain. It comes in several different forms: creams, pills, sprays and ointments. Almost every health food and holistic pharmacy in the U.S. and Canada carries some version of Arnica. It's not very expensive and - a big plus - it seems to work well on pets, too.

I'm not sure about the shelf life of this product so I just replace it each time I go on a long cruise. I buy two tubes - one for Kip's kit and another for my two-legged crew kit. Be sure to check with your health care provider before using this or any of the products/ remedies mentioned in *Doggy on Deck*.

Rapid Relief® by HTB works much like Arnica although Rapid Relief® can be applied not only to sore or bruised skin, it can be applied directly to open wounds. Healing time is much faster when this blend of essential oils is applied. As with any holistic treatment, you need to reapply Rapid Relief® every few hours until the healing is well on its way.

My dog gets anxious when we leave the dock.
What can I give her to help calm her?

Rescue Remedy®, a Bach Flower Remedy, is a combination of five different flower essences. It is designed to help calm users in emergencies or in the stress of everyday life. Doses vary but just a few drops under the tongue or in your dog's water will help to calm her anxiety.

Serene®, another product by HTB, is a blend of twenty-one essential oils. It comes in two forms: a liquid concentrate and a spray bottle. Both are extremely useful for calming anxiety due to grief, shock, trauma and insomnia. Serene® is similar in function to Rescue Remedy®. I've used both remedies on Kip, myself, various crew members and guests aboard my boat. I like both Rescue Remedy® and Serene® although I think Serene® works faster and the results are more obvious.

RESOURCES

Natural remedies

Here, There and Beyond, Inc.: As I mentioned above, this is a small company and each bottle is carefully hand-blended and inspected. I like their products a great deal - both for Kip and for myself. I've turned a bunch of folks onto this line and so far no one has been disappointed. www.oils4U.com

Bug Off Garlic Chewables™: These tablets were developed to help shield against fleas, ticks, mosquitoes, etc. They need to be given in daily doses as they are only effective for 24 hours per dose. This is just one (of maybe 50) brands available. www.springtimeinc.com

Flea Away® Natural Flea Powder: This is the Diatomaceous earth powder I mentioned above. An 8 oz. bottle covers 4,000 square feet of carpet (that is a lot of boat!). www.onlynaturalpet.com

Bach Flower Remedies-Rescue Remedy®: Liquid and cream forms can be found in most health food stores in the United States and throughout Europe. You can also order it online from www.ihealthtree.com.

www.swansonvitiams.com: This online retailer carries a fairly extensive selection of almost all of the holistic remedies I can think of. Their prices are extremely competitive.

Books on natural health care for your dog

Homeopathic Remedies for Dogs by Geoffry Llewellyn $19.95
www.amazon.com

Vet on Call: The Best Home Remedies for Keeping Your Dog Healthy by the editors of *Pets: Part of the Family* $14.95
www.amazon.com

CHANGES IN LATITUDES

Is it necessary to get our dog tattooed or
micro-chipped if we plan to cruise in the tropics?

If you're going to travel with your dog, you must get her permanently identified. First, because you love the little (or huge) furball and you don't want to lose her: If she gets lost, you want someone to find her and then find you. Second, places like Australia, New Zealand, Hawaii and even some of the smaller island territories require the permanent identification of pets. Even if you don't plan to travel with your pet, why take the risk of losing her to a pound, a research lab or to some unscrupulous pet snatching villain? Getting your dog permanently identified is like getting her vaccinated - just do it. Right now.

There are two ways of permanently identifying your dog: tattooing and micro-chipping. Tattooing is the oldest method and although it sounds permanent, it isn't, really. Tattoos can fade or get stretched and distorted over time. They are often placed in inconspicuous places (like under a hind leg) and fur can and often does grow over them. There is a possibility for infection from the tattooing process; however, if you have it applied by a vet or other professional animal health care provider, the chances of this are slim. The process is supposed to be painless, but I've chatted with several friends who sport tattoos and when they aren't showing off, they tell me it hurts like *#+?@&! For the reasons I've listed, I don't recommend tattooing.

A more modern method and the method most vets and lawmakers suggest is the process of micro-chipping. Micro-chips are tiny gizmos about the size of a grain of rice. Your vet will inject the chip under your dog's skin using a hypodermic needle. Then you and your vet will register with one of two companies (depending which chip your vet uses). After that, if your dog is lost, any vet (or customs agent) worldwide can simply scan your dog and find out any and all the information necessary to reunite you and your best buddy. Of course, this won't work in places where there are no vets, or where the technology is grossly outdated. However, it will work whenever you are trying to fly or cruise into any major port of call, anywhere in the world. Most countries do not require micro-chipping in order to import pets - yet. It is only a matter of time before these laws change. The process isn't painful (except for the initial needle prick) and is relatively inexpensive. Registering costs under $20.

There are two major companies currently offering micro-chipping for dogs. The first is HomeAgain. You can purchase a kit and either do it yourself (again, for under $20) or have your vet do it during your pre-cruise exam. I'm a bit squeamish around needles so I asked our vet to handle the details. HomeAgain is owned by the American Kennel Club (AKC).

The second company, Avid, is used by the Canadian Kennel Club (CKC). You can't buy single units with this system; you have to have Avid chips inserted by a vet. Both systems work the same way, with an easily accessible number available year round, 24/7.

What about dog tags?

Dog tags - in addition to micro-chipping - are a must when cruising. The information on your dog's tags will be slightly different from what is printed on his land-based tags. Cruising tags should be engraved with the name of your pet, your vessel name, the VHF channel you monitor, your call sign (if applicable) and your SailMail address (or other onboard phone or internet information). Make sure you select stainless steel tags because plastic can fade and crack from exposure to saltwater. The hooks holding tags to the collar should also be stainless steel because other metals rust.

I met another cruiser who shared two nifty dog identification tricks with me. The first is to have your dog's collar embroidered with vital information. How simple is that! My mother is fond of sending Kip special collars as gifts. He has Christmas bells embroidered on one, tiny blue sailboats on another and several with his full name in red, white and blue threads. Next time, I'll ask her to have the name of our boat and the hailing channel embroidered instead of those shamrocks she'd been planning.

The second cool trick is to use slide tags instead of dangling tags. These can't get lost (unless the entire collar is lost), and can be engraved on both sides just like regular tags. They don't knock against each other so you don't hear that little tinkling sound every time your dog moves her head (I sort of like the sound, but many folks don't).

Is saltwater bad for my dog's paws?

If you intend to cruise the world, plan on being black and blue, sick, tired, unable to eat, sunburnt, frozen and dirty. You'll get lines around your eyes from squinting. You'll get rashes, and the skin on your feet will crack. And what about Fido? He'll get bumped around a bit too. Dogs get sunburnt and seasick, and yes, constant exposure to saltwater will cause his paws to crack and bleed.

If you've ever gone on a snowy hike, or cross-country skied with a dog, you'll know about ice collecting between his toes. It irritates dogs and they'll stop running, sit down and bite at the ice. The same happens with saltwater. It builds up between the toes, leaving salt crystals clinging to fur. The salt irritates the webs between the dog's toes, causing the skin to crack and bleed.

When this first happened to Kip, the white fur on his paws was pink with fresh blood. Needless to say, I freaked. I tried using salves, creams, lotions and various ointments. First aid treatments, such as rubbing Neosporin® on the pads of his feet at night helped, but the next day he'd be right back in the water again. Finally, as I've learned time and time again, the simplest solution turned out to be the best solution.

Captain George and I found a flat, plastic tub – the kind you might use for washing dishes. We filled it about halfway with fresh water and placed it next to the boarding ladder. Each time Kip came aboard, we made him walk through the tub. He resisted the first couple of times, but after that, he got the hang of it and stepped into the tub on his own. He developed a ritual for himself: One front paw in, then the next. Then the first front paw out, followed by the second. Repeat the process with the hind paws. Done. A quick fresh water rinse for each paw, each time he came out of the water, cleared the saltwater problem. His paws healed rapidly and the problem of salt on his paws was resolved.

Will the saltwater damage my dog's coat?

Yes. But not like you'd expect it to. *Your* hair will lighten if you cruise in the tropics. Unless you keep your head covered all day, every day, you'll find your hair color goes two shades lighter almost immediately. My hair color usually changes from auburn to strawberry blond in less than a month. Kip's fur lightens as well. But, more interesting (and troublesome), he develops dreadlocks from the saltwater and wind. Unless he gets a close clip, long yellow dreads hang from Kip's head and his shoulders. He becomes my little Rasta Dog. Other people think he looks cute, but I spend a great deal of time cutting twisted clumps from my pooch.

If you don't have a mega-yacht or a huge capacity water-maker, chances are you won't be hosing your dog down with fresh water every time she gets out of the sea. So, while a low pan of fresh water will serve to rinse her paws, what about the issue of matting and tangling that comes with constant exposure to wind and salt? Simple answer? Brushing. Brushing, brushing and more brushing. This will slow the process, but you still may need to cut out a dread-lock from time to time. In the <u>Resources</u> at the end of this section, I've listed several companies that provide dog grooming supplies to professional groomers and veterinarians. Shop online for the best selection. Some of the larger chain stores carry these products as well, although the versions designed for the general consumer market are

78

not as "heavy duty" as those designed for professional groomers. I suggest you buy the sturdiest products available. Put a few drops of oil on your grooming tools to keep them from rusting, and store them in Ziploc bags.

Our dog sheds a lot: Will that be a problem on the boat?

Shedding is not only annoying (it's something we pet lovers seem to just "put up with") it can actually be hazardous on a vessel. On land I keep sticky tape rollers everywhere: The glove compartment, under the bathroom sinks, in my desk drawer at work. I even keep one in my briefcase for one last "fur removal" before heading into a client or faculty meeting. Even then, the worst thing that can happen if I miss rolling my suit is points off in the fastidious grooming department. *Not so on the boat.* Two incidents alerted me to the importance of keeping dog fur under control while at sea.

I was crewing for a friend, Rob, aboard his small sloop. Rob, his girlfriend Kelly, and his dog, Max, plus Kip and I shared ten great days dinking around in the Canadian Gulf Islands. Max is a long-haired Husky mix. Kip, as you know, is a fluffy Border Collie mix. The two dogs got along great and when they romped onboard, the fur flew.

One day, the sky turned from powder to gun-barrel-blue. The winds ratcheted up from a pleasant 15 knots to a fluky 30 gusting to 40. The heavens opened and rain poured down. As the winds increased and the water churned, Kelly's color shifted from a healthy glow to a greenish grey. Despite our urgings to stay above decks, she insisted on going below to lie in her bunk. She took the two dogs for support. Rob and I stayed on deck taking turns at the helm. We were motor sailing with a small storm sail and triple reefed main. It wasn't a particularly dangerous situation but we were fairly uncomfortable. I huddled on the bench in my yellow follies watching Rob handle the wheel. Absentmindedly, I glanced down. Rob was standing in swirling water. It had almost reached the tops of his rubber boots.

"Rob!" Yelling above the wind, I pointed at the small, choppy lake forming in the cockpit. Rob's eyes widened; he swore and then yelled at me to grab the wheel. He sloshed through the water and, carefully removing just the top two companionway slots, headed below to check the thru holes.

"They're open!" He popped back up the companionway. "Something must be blocking the drain up here!" Well, of course you know it wasn't a wad of leaves or newspaper blocking the cockpit drains; it was dog fur. Dog fur mats into a tight felt-like material. Plunging his arm into the swirling water Rob scooped up the block. I followed suit on the second hole and within minutes the cockpit had drained. It was a lesson that ended okay but the situation could have been much more serious.

Another time, on my own boat, I discovered a small bit of fur-felt about the size of a pencil eraser clogging one of my water lines. It took me a long time to trace the lines and I never did figure out how the fur got in there. Again, the situation at the time wasn't serious but it reminded me of the importance of keeping dog fur to a minimum onboard. And the simple solution, again, is brushing. Pick a time - while having the first cup of coffee, or maybe that sundowner - to give your dog a daily brushing. It will reduce the shedding, keep the boat safe, and keep her coat smooth and tangle free. It will also give you both some gentle bonding time.

Do dogs get seasick?

Yes. At some point, everyone at sea gets seasick. And as Kip McSnip and my mother discovered during an afternoon sail in the Caribbean, misery *loves* company..

My mother has never been a dog-lover. In fact, she's had a sort of phobia about dogs all her life. I can remember her grabbing my sister and me and dragging us to the other side of the street if faced with even so much as a toy poodle. She's not a big boating enthusiast either. Although she's happy to travel aboard big - REALLY BIG - boats, she's not the "sleep in the v-berth" sort. Because of this, I was rather surprised when she announced she'd like to fly to St. Thomas and do a little sailing with Captain George and me.

"Mom, we've got the dog and cat aboard, you know."

"Well, I like that old cat."

"But Mom, you know you're not all that fond of boats. Or dogs."

"Nonsense, your father and I went out on boats quite a bit when we were young."

I sighed, "what about the dog, Mom? The puppy. He's got to stay on the boat with us, and he's full of energy. It's a small boat, mom." Mother was determined. One of her Red Hat group excursions overseas had been cancelled - something about political unrest. She had the time off, the refunded airfare, and no place to go. She was coming for a visit.

"It will be okay," Captain George assured me, "We'll stay in close - maybe just go to the BVI's. She'll adjust to the boat - she'll be fine." I wasn't so sure. I watched Kip rolling around on the foredeck, his snout wedged deep into a plastic peanut butter jar. It wasn't mom adjusting to the boat that had me worried.

Mom stayed in a hotel the first couple of days. We window-shopped the expensive jewelry stores lining the main street of St. Thomas and ate iced shrimp salads in open-air cafés on the water-front. Captain George stayed on *Reve* with the critters while Mom and I booked a ferry to St. John. The goal was to get her adjusted to the feel of open water during the short trip between the two islands. As the aging vessel belched diesel and lurched to a start, I held my breath and hoped for the best. Within minutes Mom had met several other ladies seated on the top deck and soon became engaged in a spirited conversation about the re-emerging popularity of hats. I'm not sure if she even noticed the boat's motion as the ferry chugged through ocean swells. I exhaled.

St. John bustled with art galleries and hand-painted clothing stores. Upscale restaurants offered chilled chardonnay and conch fritters. Island flowers and parrots burst with color. Determined to "not miss a thing," Mother flitted from shop to shop gaily chatting with gallery owners and fellow tourists. An afternoon rain squall caught us outside, on the beach. Drenched to the bone, Mom laughed as I photographed her emptying rainwater from her handbag. I began to let my guard down. Maybe this would be okay. The real test would come the next morning.

While Mom and I played tourist, Captain George had been watching the weather. He met us at the ferry landing when we returned, and over dinner he announced that we should leave for the BVI's early the next morning. Mother was excited – her first sailboat ride.

Mom met us at the dock at daybreak. Bless her heart; she had dressed in blue and white stripes, wore new white tennis shoes and sported a bright red baseball cap. She'd packed a swimsuit, tanning lotion and a point-and-shoot camera. Mom was ready to go sailing.

The first couple of hours went well. I ran interference between the puppy and my mother, keeping him on the port side while she stayed to starboard. Kip was eager to inspect this new person, but Mom shooed him away and politely kept her distance. As the sun climbed higher, Mom seemed quite happy. She decided to go below and change into her swimsuit.

"Don't spend much time down there," Captain George warned her. "It's easy to get woozy below decks. And, we're coming up to the pass – it gets a bit rough in there." I don't know if Mom was heeding the Captain's suggestion or if haste became a necessity, but she changed clothes and was back on deck – gulping fresh air – in record time.

"Oh my," she gasped, fanning her face with her hand. "You were right, George. I do feel a bit woozy."

My mother was more than a bit woozy. In the short time she'd been below her skin had turned a pale green. The green you'd get if you mixed a hint of mildew with a dash of mold. Her breathing was short and high. A classic case of *mal de mer*.

"Come hold the helm," Captain George instructed. But Mom wouldn't move from the bench. She pushed her back into the cockpit bulkhead, gritted her teeth and tried to focus through glazed eyes. Captain George and I exchanged glances. He motioned toward the companionway. We kept two "cures" for seasickness aboard: Candied ginger and ice cold Heineken®. Despite conventional wisdom about avoiding alcohol when ill, Captain George swore by his beer cure. I leaned toward the ginger method. Mom could take her pick.

I headed down the companionway steps but stopped when I heard a low moaning sound. Kip was lying on the cockpit sole, pressed flat against the cool fiberglass. Even with all that fur, he'd taken on the same moldy green coloring as my mom. In between his gasping pants, he alternated between moans, howls and whimpers. The sound was both eerie and pathetic. I looked from the puppy up to Captain George. The captain simply shrugged his shoulders – beer probably wouldn't work for a dog. We were both at a loss. Then Mom did something I never thought I'd see. And, I would think I had made it up if Captain George hadn't had the presence of mind to snap a couple photos.

"Oh, you poor baby." Mom actually cooed despite her own

misery. "You better come and sit with Grandma. She'll take care of you." Then she patted the bench. Kip looked up and rolled his eyes. I didn't think he had the strength to move so I scooped him up and stretched him out next to my mother. She reached over and pulled him half way onto her lap. "See now," Mom stroked Kip's head, "you and Grandma will pull through this together." Kip looked up at her with sad, brown eyes and sealed the bond. For the next two hours Mom and the puppy comforted each other while George and I sailed our little boat to the island of Jost Van Dyke.

What should I do if my dog gets seasick?

Mal de mer retreats quickly once the afflicted parties touch terra firma. By dinner time both Mom and Kip were in the pink. They remain close buddies to this day because of their adventure together. The ocean doesn't play favorites; moms, grandmas, dogs – at some point everyone gets seasick.

There is nothing wimpy about getting motion sickness. Even the crustiest of old salts can remember a time when the roll of the ocean got the better of him. However, except in the most extreme cases, seasickness doesn't kill anyone. Rarely lasting longer than three days, it eventually runs its course and leaves. The treatments are the same for both dogs and people. The best thing to do to prevent a queasy stomach is to remain on deck in the fresh air and to look out toward the horizon. Make sure you have food in your belly – the kind of food depends on the individual. Many sailors prefer bland foods such as oatmeal or granola. Some go for spicy or salty foods. For dogs, I recommend just offering their regular food. Not a lot of it, but enough to steady a rolling stomach. Drink lots of fresh water. Keep busy and think of England. If none of that works, then use the remedies listed below.

There are several remedies (not including Captain George's beer cure) that will help calm the symptoms of seasickness. Some remedies, such as the Scopolamine patch, are intended for people and should not be used on your pet. All of the remedies I'll discuss here can be safely used for both you and your pet. Purchase these herbs and other items before you leave on your cruise as some of them can be difficult to find in more remote areas.

Candied ginger is my favorite remedy. I buy it in bulk at health food stores. You only need a nibble at a time so I buy a pound and that lasts forever. I keep it in a Tupperware container in the galley and tell all my crew members to help themselves. It's not expensive, tastes good and, in my experience, really works. Just one small piece at the first sign of queasiness and all is well.

You can feed your dog ginger snaps or ginger biscuits. I've included a recipe for homemade ginger cookies at the end of this section. You can also put powdered ginger in capsules and give these to your dog in a bit of cheese. Most health food stores carry powdered ginger and empty capsules. Sometimes you can find ginger capsules already prepared. Another ginger delivery system is tea. Pour boiling water over a couple slices of raw ginger and let them steep. Strain the tea and let it cool before giving it to your pet. You can pour it over a tasty bit of food, soak a dog biscuit in it or, the best method, allow your dog to just drink it. One sailor suggested putting drops of ginger essential oil on a pet's bedding. I'm not sure if that will be as effective as ingesting the root, but it certainly wouldn't hurt anything, and it would lend a pleasant smell to your boat.

Fenugreek and peppermint are two more herbs that work much like ginger. You can make teas from both, and both have essential oils. For people, a piece of hard peppermint candy will do in a pinch but refined sugar isn't highly recommended for dogs. The best way to administer these herbs is to brew them into teas. Let them cool as you would with the ginger tea before giving them to your dog. Bagged peppermint tea is readily available, but you may have to purchase dried fenugreek and brew your own tea.

Raw honey helps to calm upset stomachs and can be drizzled on food or treats. This should not be given to animals or people with heart problems, however. Raw honey is part of an especially useful trick when traveling with kids. A peanut butter and honey sandwich seems to prep little tummies for the motion of the ocean. It's simple and gets some food in them. It works for dogs too as all dogs seem to love peanut butter.

I've discussed Rescue Remedy® and Serene® earlier. Both can be used to calm anxious crew members (again, both two and four-legged), and both are completely natural so you don't need to worry about noxious chemistry. Rescue Remedy® is a Bach Flower remedy. Made from distilled water and flower essences, these remedies are safe to take and to give to your animal. You can put four drops directly in your dog's mouth (halve that for a very small dog) or put a few drops in his water bowl. If you haven't used Bach Flower remedies before you might want to visit almost any large health food store and ask for information about these popular remedies.

Serene® is a blend of essential oils and should not be taken internally. Instead, either rub Serene® concentrate on your pet's fur or put a couple of drops in your palms, then rub your pet's feet. You can also squirt the Serene® spray on your dog's fur. Sometimes I squirt a little Serene® in the cabin or in the cockpit because it smells pleasant and instantly calms my crew. A calm crew is a safer, happier crew.

Personally, I don't use over-the-counter seasick meds because they make me too drowsy to be effective in emergencies. And I don't give them to Kip because I'd rather rely on more natural remedies like those described above. You can, however, move to more aggressive treatments if the natural remedies don't work for you. Dramamine®, a common over-the-counter treatment for motion sickness, works for pets just as it does for people. Give medium to large dogs (30 pounds and up), between 25 to 50 milligrams and small dogs (under 30 pounds) about 12.5 milligrams. You'll need to administer this at least an hour before leaving the dock. Avoid this medication if you or your pet have bladder problems or glaucoma.

Benadryl® also works much the same on pets as it does on people. It's generally administered as an antihistamine to alleviate acute inflammatory and allergic reactions to things such as bee stings, insect bites and coral scrapes. It also has a strong anti-nausea side effect making it useful to curb seasickness. There are several other side effects, so be sure to read, keep and follow the instructions included with the drug. I carry this in my ship's medical kit in order to treat severe allergic reactions; however, again, for seasickness, I stick to the more benign and natural remedies. BE SURE TO CHECK WITH YOUR OWN VET BEFORE ADMINISTERING THIS OR ANY OTHER DRUG.

Don't dogs get hot in the tropics?

Everyone gets hot in the tropics. Isn't that one of the reasons we go there? Still, it's a good question. We need to help our four-legged buddies stay cool whether we're cruising in paradise or driving our cars to the mall. Obviously, on a hot day in our home port, we don't leave our pets in the car - even with the windows rolled down. We leave them in the air-conditioned house and take them walking around the neighborhood in the evening. But what should we do if we're anchored out in a lagoon in the Tuamotoes or strolling down a sandy beach on St. Croix?

The third time Kip and I cruised Mexico, he spent most of his time panting. He hadn't done that very often on earlier trips so I though it was just another sign of his advancing age. That is, until a friend of mine, another sailor, compared Kip's silky fur to a down jacket.

"I don't know why he wasn't bothered before," my friend commented, "but he sure looks hot now." Maybe she had a point. I got on the Cruisers' Net the next morning and made a request for information about finding dog groomers. I don't think I've ever had a question that couldn't be answered by someone on a local cruiser's radio net. Within minutes of making the request, two cruisers radioed back with the name of a local woman who did dog grooming. By early afternoon, Kip and I were wandering the streets of Zihuatanejo, looking for the woman's shop. When we located the groomer I used my eight words of Spanish to explain what we needed. A beautiful, young Mexican woman listened carefully and then told me (in perfect English) to go have lunch and come back after siesta.

When I returned, three hours later, I didn't recognize my buddy. He'd gone from an elegant, long-haired beauty to a scrawny, almost

87

hairless, street gang-looking mutt. And, he pranced - yes, pranced - out of the shop and into the afternoon sunlight. He'd lost a heavy coat and gained a new lease on life.

There are other things you can do, besides a coat trimming, to keep your pooch cool. Providing shade is critical. My boat has a fully enclosed cockpit with panels that open all around for air circulation. If your boat doesn't have cover, you can copy my friend, Bob, and erect a colorful beach umbrella. When Bob pops the tops on a couple of cold beers and opens his "shade tree," his cockpit turns into an instant fiesta!

If you have the luxury of having an ice maker or freezer aboard, slide a couple ice cubes in your dog's water dish. For a special hot day treat make ice cubes out of water and no-salt beef or chicken bouillon. They are the equivalent of popsicles for dogs and are just as much fun for pets as ice cream is for people.

I keep a spray bottle of water in the reefer and send Kip into a happy trance with cool spritzings. Add a few drops of Serene® into the water and your crew - all of them - will be both calm and cool - even on the hottest days at sea.

A final trick, one used by the military when deploying working dogs overseas, is the Canine Cool Coat® by the Ray Allen Company. This vest contains a UniPak® of non-toxic coolant. You just put the UniPak® in ice water or a freezer for a half hour and then slip it into the vest. It will keep your dog cool for up to two hours.

Do dogs get sunburned?

They can. Especially light-haired, pink-nosed dogs. Even dark-haired dogs, after a close clip or summer hair cut, are susceptible to sunburn. Just like people, dogs can get burned, sometimes seriously, from overexposure to the sun. Generally the burn will peel and go away, but in severe cases, sunburns can turn into infected lesions or even cancer. The easiest way to deal with this is simply keep your dog out of the sun during the hottest part of the day. Take walks in the cool of the mornings or evenings. And if you're on a beach at noon, make sure your dog has shade and plenty of water.

What about using doggy sunscreen?

There is an ongoing debate in the veterinary community about the wisdom of using "people sunscreen" on dogs. Dogs will probably lick the stuff off - almost immediately - and there is a chance of a negative reaction to the ingredients in the skincare product. Although some products are harmless, even for human infants, it's too risky for my tastes. There are companies that manufacture sunscreen specifically formulated for dogs. These are a safer bet. Still, the best treatment is prevention. Use common sense and keep Fido as protected as you would a human baby.

What can I do if my dog gets dehydrated?

Dehydration can be extremely serious for dogs as well as for people. Lack of water in any climate can contribute to dehydration but it's especially important that your pet receives plenty of clean, fresh water while traveling in warmer climates. Sun exposure and seasickness can cause a drop in fluid levels. Diarrhea and vomiting can also speed the loss of fluids. Dehydration, or lack of fluids, can cause disorientation, confusion, exhaustion and eventually death. Common symptoms include appetite loss, depression, a dry mouth and foul breath. To conduct a simple test for dehydration just pull up on the skin on your dog's back. It should flatten back naturally without your pet needing to shake it down. If the skin remains up, in a tight ridge shape, it's highly likely your buddy suffers from dehydration.

Kip suffered from dehydration once after a particularly grueling plane ride. He could barely move and lay still, completely flattened. I couldn't get him to drink and had no way of reaching veterinary help. I filled a sport bottle with cool water and, pulling his gums back, squirted a slow stream of water into his mouth. I'm not sure if he swallowed the water or not, but I kept a steady dribble of water running across his gums and into his mouth for several minutes. Then, I repeated the process every thirty minutes. It took about four hours of administering water like this until he eventually perked up.

You may need to do something like this if your dog has been sick (vomiting or experiencing diarrhea), or if he's simply too list-less to drink. If you need to give your dog water this way, be sure to squirt slowly as too much water too fast can cause choking or even more vomiting. If your pet is alert and interested enough to handle licking an ice cube, give him one made with beef or chicken bouillon. This is an excellent method of getting water (and nutrition) into your pet slowly.

Replacing electrolytes is an important element in getting your pet back to good health. You can purchase expensive electrolyte replacement formulas or you can use Pedialyte®, a formula for children. Pedialyte® is available from almost any drug store in the U.S., and you might want to take some with you. Be careful about buying it outside the U.S. Read the label to insure that you are buying the latest formula as older versions contained aspartame.

Even healthy dogs can get dehydrated quickly when exposed to too much sun or when doing strenuous exercise in high temperatures. Remember to pack a bowl and bottle of water for your dog when you go hiking or exploring new territory. In many remote areas it's easier to find cold beer than potable water. Unless your four-legged buddy can belly up to the bar, it's up to you to provide the refreshments. You can pack a folding water dish (see the Resources at the end of this chapter for places to find travel dishes for dogs) or just take a lightweight bowl with you. Before I discovered folding water bowls I poked a hole in the rim of a small Tupperware dish and clipped it to my belt with a carabineer.

It's easy to become dehydrated when we're playing, hiking and exploring. It's easy to forget to pack water and even easier to forget to drink enough water along the way. But dehydration can be serious and we, as responsible cruisers and pet owners, simply have to make the effort to remember to provide shade, plenty of water and a cooling off time during any activities undertaken in high temperatures. We need to do this for ourselves and, especially, for our furry friends.

Do dogs suffer from heat stroke?

Unfortunately, dogs don't handle the heat as well as people. Even if you do use the methods described in the section on dehydration, you may have to deal with heat stroke at some point in your travels. Heat stroke is most likely to occur when the temperature is extremely high and your dog is in any kind of unshaded or confined area. Short-nosed dogs, like Pugs and some Bulldogs, are more likely to suffer from heat stroke than other breeds. Muzzled dogs are extremely vulnerable to heat stroke as well.

How can I tell if my dog is suffering from heat stroke?

There are distinct symptoms of heat stroke. Your dog will start panting with noisy, frantic breathing. His gums and tongue will turn bright red and he may vomit or have bloody diarrhea. He may appear to be drunk - staggering and toppling over. Heat stroke can kill - quickly - and needs to be treated immediately.

Get your dog to a cooler environment at once. An easy procedure is simply immersing him in cool water. If you have a wash down hose aboard, hose him down. Pour a bucket of water over him if you have to. The main point is to cool your dog's temperature as rapidly as possible. Simply getting water down his throat won't do it. You need to cool his entire body and get him into a cool, shady place immediately. As his body temperature lowers, he'll become less agitated and his tongue and gums will return to their normal color. Then just stay with him and keep him quiet and calm as long as possible. By the time the sun sets and the temperature drops, your buddy should be back to his happy, frisky self.

Will my dog get worms while we're cruising in the tropics?

Your dog can come in contact with worms (parasites that live off host animals) whether you are trampsing the jungles of Brazil or taking a stroll through the botanical gardens in Vancouver. Puppies and dogs can be infected with five major kinds of worms. The most common worms found in canines are roundworms and hookworms (commonly found in puppies) and whipworms, tapeworms, and heartworms (more often found in mature dogs). If left untreated, worms can cause serious illness and even death; however, modern veterinary medicine has made it possible to treat, and in most cases prevent, the growth of worms in dogs. I'll give you a brief overview on the subject and offer some suggestions of meds you'll want to carry onboard. For an excellent and more thorough discussion of canine worms and their treatment, visit the website for University of Georgia's College of Veterinary Medicine at www.uga.edu.

Roundworms and Hookworms

Roundworms feed on undigested food left in a dog's intestine. Female dogs can pass these to their babies during pregnancy, hence the propensity for roundworms to show up in puppies. Hookworms also feed off dogs' intestines and because their teeth are sharp and "hook-like" they cause the intestine to bleed. Like roundworms, puppies can contract these worms from the mother dog. Dogs can also get both of these kinds of worms by eating worm eggs found on the ground.

Heartworms, Whipworms and Tapeworms

The first of these three live in dogs' hearts and blood vessels – and so the name, heartworms. These are particularly troublesome for cruisers as they are spread by mosquitoes. Mosquitoes get infected by biting infected dogs and then spread the worms to uninfected dogs.

As with roundworms and hookworms, dogs usually get whipworms from eating the eggs left by an infected dog. These worms attack the intestines and cause bleeding.

Tapeworms are passed along by fleas. A flea eats a tapeworm egg and then a dog eats the flea (while trying to prevent the pain and itching caused by the flea's biting). The dog now has the tapeworm egg. Tapeworms are long and flat and absorb nutrition through their skin rather than through a mouth. All five forms of worm are disgusting, can cause illness and death in your dog, and need to be destroyed.

Your veterinarian will check your pet for worms during her annual check-up, but in the meantime you can keep an eye out for obvious signs of worms by noticing your dog's stools. In many cases you can actually see the worms in the feces.

There are several kinds of medicines to treat dogs for worms. Some of these are available over the counter, others require prescription. To prevent worms you can - and absolutely should - treat your dog monthly with medications like Revolution®. It's best to find out if your dog has worms before beginning any kind of treatment or prevention regime. Try to make your pre-trip veterinary appointment in plenty of time for test results to be returned and for your pet to be well into the first month of treatment before you set sail.

We haven't spayed our dog; what if she has puppies "out there?"

Do you seriously want to put your beloved pet and yourselves through pregnancy and a litter of puppies at sea? Let's say you have perfect weather and everything goes smoothly and the puppies and mother dog are fine - then what? What will you do with all those little dogs? What if you travel to a country requiring a quarantine? Are you going to set enough of your cruising kitty aside to provide for, say, seven dogs? Ouch. And if you are allowed to land with your menagerie, will you be giving the puppies away? There are many countries where domestic pets are not treated with the level of care you might want for your pet's offspring.

I tried saving a litter of puppies while visiting a small island a while back. We were docked close to a village where several dogs ran and played. No one claimed them as pets but they seemed healthy and happy. Almost every cruiser who dropped the hook adopted them as temporary family members. But apparently someone in the area didn't appreciate the local dogs. One morning a couple of cruisers out for an early jog found the bodies of four of them. The animals had been poisoned. A female dog who'd given birth just two days before was among the dead.

When I learned what had happened, I gathered the orphaned litter into a plastic tub and carried the newborns back to my boat. With the help of other cruisers I purchased baby formula from a small store in the village and set up a feeding schedule. We tried everything we could to save those babies. But they didn't make it. They screamed and cried all night long until one by one, they died. The experience was hard on all of us and left a sad note in our log books.

Here's my personal opinion on this question: Just don't do it. If you want your dog to enjoy a healthier, longer life, then spay or neuter your pet.

RESOURCES

Serene® by Here, There and Beyond, Inc. www.oils4u.com

Rescue Remedy®, a Bach Flower Remedy: www.bachflower.com
and www.ihealthtree.com

Peppermint, fenugreek, ginger: (dried, teas, powders and oils) www.
mountainroseherbs.com

The Cool Coat
Canine Cool Coat® Ray Allen Company. www.rayallen.com

Micro-chip kits
For the HomeAgain™ do-it-yourself kits, go to Countryside Vet Supply www.countrysidevetsupply.com An excellent site explaining
how to give your pet injections is www.terrierman.com/vaccines

For information on the Avid Systems™ go to www.microchip.com.
Again, these must be injected by a vet.

Tags
For custom embroidered collars go to www.pettags.com. This
company also makes regular dangle tags. Be sure to specify stainless
steel when ordering tags.

Slide collar tags come in three sizes for large, medium and small dogs.
Try www.gotags.com for the best deals on these tags.

Clippers, brushes and de-shedding combs
Oscar Frank Universal Slicker Brushes: These are a simple, old stand-
by in the dog grooming world. Mostly plastic construction. They
can be purchased at almost any pet supply store. Most large chain
stores like Wal-Mart and Target carry these as well.

Safari by Coastal This is a complete line of grooming products designed for home use. Go to www.coastalpet.com for a retailer in your area.

Paw Brothers: A complete line of grooming aids for both home and professional use. Take a look at the Coat Breakers (for removing mats and tangles without losing much of the dog's coat). This company also offers several de-matting tools and a wide selection of nail clippers. Products are constructed of stainless steel. Call them toll free at 800-525-7387 or you can order their products at www.RyansPet.com.

Bamboo De-shedding Comb: Just one of several brands offering de-shedding tools. The nice thing about this tool is the compact, easy to grip shape. Again, go to www.RyansPet.com for a look at this and other models. The prices at www.RyansPet.com are lower than I've found elsewhere. If you'd like a paper catalogue listing (literally) thousands of pet grooming aids, call them toll free at 1-800-525-7387.

Folding Dog Dishes: www.thepetonline.com

Sunscreens formulated for dogs
PET Sunscreen SPF 15 www.funstufffordogs.com

Pethealth Factor 30 Sunblock in a cream formula. www.ultimateanimals.co.uk

Pethealth Sun Block This comes in a stick version and is waterproof. www.ultimateanimals.co.uk

Old Fashioned Ginger Snaps
(good for ALL the members of your crew)

These keep a long time so you can make a large batch before leaving and enjoy them all the way across an ocean! This recipe makes about 100 small cookies.

Preheat oven to 350°F

Ingredients:
1 cup molasses	1/2 teaspoon baking soda
1/2 cup shortening (or butter)	1 tablespoon dried ginger
3 1/4 cups flour	1 1/2 teaspoon salt

Directions:
Sift dry ingredients together and set aside in a large bowl. Heat molasses almost to boiling over a medium heat. Pour molasses over shortening in a separate bowl. Stir in dry ingredients. Mix the ingredients by hand until it forms a dough. Divide dough into four parts and work on one part at a time. Keep the remaining parts in the refrigerator until you need them. Roll the dough as thin as possible and cut with small cookie cutters. (I have a bone shaped cookie cutter.) Work quickly so the dough will not dry out. Place on a greased baking sheet. Bake until crispy - about 8 to 10 minutes.

OFFICIAL HOO HA

Where can we take my dog?

Remember my neighbor, Mrs. Glubner? She was the first to tell me I couldn't take a dog to the tropics. At the time, she was thinking of the heat, but if she'd known about Customs and quarantine laws, she would have expanded her lecture. The questions covered in this section are important and almost anyone contemplating a long journey with a pet wonders about them. These serious questions are also the most difficult to answer. They are problematic because the rules vary from country to country, and individual countries change their own rules without warning. Government agencies creating the rules don't communicate with each other, so what you learn as the "official law of the land" from one governmental source may contradict what you learn from another agency in that same country. You may complete every single form, pay every required fee, and have all your papers in order only to find that an admitting customs agent has never heard of these forms. They mean nothing, and you must start all over with new forms and new fees. Or sometimes, if your luck holds, you can slip the agent a "gift" and be on your way. There is confusion and disorganization at every stage of the game.

At this point, you might think I'm referring to small, third world countries. Nope: Some of the most discombobulated snafus Kip and I have encountered have been right here in the good old U.S. of A. My dog and I have flown or sailed together into the United States from Antigua, Canada, French Polynesia, Mexico and the U.S. Virgin Islands. Each time the process to enter our home country has been different. Kip was more welcomed by officials in French Polynesia (traditionally extremely strict regarding the importation of animals) than he has been flying into Los Angeles. He was scrutinized arriving in Seattle and ignored landing in Detroit. To be completely honest, the more I cruise, the more I believe there are no real systems. Each situation, place, and official gatekeeper seems unique.

I'm going to do the best I can to give you the most current information available regarding several major cruising areas. I'll tell you all the best steps you can take to prepare for most situations. And, I'll share stories of what happened to us when we traveled in those areas. However, I have to warn you, as I said above, the rules are constantly changing. My best advice to you is that you take all the steps you can to prepare, that you consult all the relevant websites listed in <u>Resources,</u> and then do one more thing: Pack a healthy dose of patience and a sense of humor. The hassles you may (probably will) encounter getting your dog into and out of various countries is just part of your cruising adventure. I hope our stories will help you prepare, at least psychologically, for what you may encounter. Make it as fun and interesting as possible by getting your ducks in a row and then be prepared to simply play the game as it unfolds.

I've gone into some detail about Canada, Hawaii, Mexico, French Polynesia and Australia because they are fairly representative of the different kinds of rules and procedures you'll encounter as you cruise the globe. Following these discussions, I've provided brief summaries of the current rules for several additional countries.

Canada

The rules regarding traveling in Canada with your dog are much like the country itself; well-organized, user-friendly, easy to understand, rational and civilized. Canada does not require that your pet be quarantined and has a fixed, clearly posted fee for inspecting animals entering the country. As of January 2007, the fees - in U.S. dollars - are $30 plus tax for the first animal and $5 plus tax for each additional animal in the same group. Most domestic pets coming from the United States are exempt from these inspections and fees. Domestic dogs may enter Canada with an Export Certificate (in either English or French) that has been signed by an official government veterinarian. An official government veterinarian is any veterinarian licensed to practice veterinary medicine. The Export Certificate must clearly identify each animal, state that rabies have not existed in the exporting country for six months prior to the shipment of the animal(s), and that all animal(s) have been in the exporting country for that same six month period. If the Export Certificate is not available, dogs may enter Canada with proof of a valid rabies vaccination issued by a licensed veterinarian. Again, each dog must be clearly identified (breed, color, weight etc.) on the documents. The trade name, serial number and expiration date of the rabies vaccine must also be noted on the proof of vaccination. This will be extremely easy for cruisers as all the information required is listed on your pet's International Health Certificate. There is no waiting period required between the time your dog is vaccinated for rabies and the time the pet is imported into Canada. Puppies under three months of age are not required to be vaccinated prior to entering Canada.

At this time the Canadian Government does not require tat-

101

too or micro-chip identification for domestic animals. There is no need to make an appointment for an inspection because a certified inspector is always on duty at the Canadian Ports of Entry. Okay – how simple is that?

So, the bottom line is to make sure you have a current rabies vaccination (International Health Certificate) to enter Canada with your dog. One more note about visiting this wonderful country with Fido: Do obey the strict leash and scoop laws. Canadians are tidy, polite people and they expect the same from their visitors.

Countries Canada Recognizes as Rabies-Free:
(for Domestic Dogs and Cats)

Antigua	New Zealand
Australia	Norway
Bahamas	St. Kitts – Nevis – Anguilla
Barbados	St. Lucia
Bermuda	St. Martin
Cayman Islands	St. Pierre et Miquelon Islands
Fiji	Sweden
Finland	Taiwan
Iceland	Turkey & Caicos Islands
Ireland (Republic of)	United Kingdom*
Jamaica	Uruguay
Japan	

*England, Scotland, Wales and Northern Ireland

Hawaii

The first thing you need to do in order to cruise the aloha waters with your four-legged crew member is to pass the Bar Exam. Hawaii's rules are obtuse, complicated, hard to understand, and extremely user-*un*friendly. However, if you carefully follow them (and you'll need to start almost a year in advance to do everything correctly), you can cruise Hawaii with as short a stay as five days in quarantine for your dog. I completely respect the desire to keep an island (or entire continent for that matter) rabies-free. But it would be nice if the rules were clear and reasonable. Here's the official "shortened and easy" checklist for taking your pet to Hawaii with a simple five days of quarantine.

CHECKLIST FOR 5-DAY-OR-LESS PROGRAM

Owners of resident Hawaii pets please use: "CHECKLIST ONLY FOR RESIDENT DOGS AND CATS ORIGINATING FROM HAWAII AND RETURNING FOR THE 5-DAY-OR-LESS PROGRAM" instead.

All steps need to be completed in order to qualify for this program.
If you are unable to meet the following requirements, your pet will undergo quarantine for up to 120 days.

Step 1 RABIES VACCINATIONS
☐ My pet has been vaccinated at least twice for rabies in its lifetime.
☐ These rabies vaccines were administered **more than 90 days** apart.
☐ The most recent rabies vaccination was done:
    ☐ Not more than 12 months prior to my pet's date of arrival in Hawaii for a 1-year rabies vaccine or;
    ☐ Not more than 36 months prior to my pet's date of arrival in Hawaii for a 3-year rabies vaccine.

The most recent rabies vaccination was also done:
☐ Not less than 90 days before my pet's date of arrival in Hawaii.

> NOTE! Two rabies vaccinations are required. The pet's most recent rabies vaccination must not have expired when your pet arrives in Hawaii. Following the most recent rabies vaccination, animals must wait at least **90** days before arriving in Hawaii. If arrival occurs before 90 days has elapsed from the most recent rabies vaccination, the animal is subject to quarantine until 90 days are completed.

☐ The date and type of vaccine must be indicated on the pet's vaccination and health certificates.

Most Recent Vaccination Date: _____ Type of vaccine (check): ☐ 1-year or ☐ 3-year
Previous Vaccination Date: _____

Step 2 MICROCHIP (Microchip number: _____)
☐ My dog or cat has an electronic microchip implanted (Required before an OIE-FAVN rabies blood test is performed).
☐ The microchip has been scanned by my veterinarian to verify that it is working and that the microchip number is correct.
☐ I understand that if scanning the implanted microchip cannot identify my pet, it will not qualify for either direct airport release or the 5-day-or-less quarantine and will be assigned to 120 days quarantine.

Step 3 OIE-FAVN RABIES BLOOD TEST
Date sample received by Kansas State University (KSU) or the DOD lab: _____
Planned Arrival Date (not less than 120 days after KSU DOD received sample)_____
Test result:_____ (passing test valid for 36 months)

☐ The day after KSU or DOD received my pet's blood sample was **not more than 36 months and not less than 120 days** before the date of arrival in Hawaii.
☐ The result of my pet's blood test was greater than or equal to 0.5 IU/ml.
☐ The test was done at an approved lab (Kansas State University or the DOD Food Analysis and Diagnostic Laboratory in Texas)
☐ I have a copy of this successful blood test result showing my pet's microchip number. Ask your submitting veterinarian for a copy of the results. Do not contact the laboratory directly.

Step 4 WAITING PERIOD – Early Arrival Means Disqualification From 5-Day or Less Quarantine or Airport Release!

> **WARNING!** Arriving anytime before the 120-day waiting period has elapsed will result in disqualification of a pet from the 5-day-or-less quarantine program and direct airport release. **IMPORTANT!** : The waiting period begins the day after KSU or DOD received the blood sample for the OIE-FAVN test. The test must also have a result ≥ 0.5 IU/ml. All pets arriving before the eligible date of entry will be quarantined and assessed $14.30 each day in addition to applicable program fees. There are no exceptions.

Following a successful OIE-FAVN test result, *animals must wait at least* **120 days** before arriving in Hawaii. If arrival occurs before 120 days has elapsed, the animal is subject to quarantine until 120 days are completed for it to then qualify for the 5-day-or-less program.

☐ I understand that if my pet has not completed the 120-day waiting period before arriving in Hawaii my pet will not qualify for either direct airport release or the 5-day-or-less quarantine program.

Step 5 DOCUMENTS

☐ I have original signature or carbon copy of rabies vaccination certificates for the **two** most recent rabies vaccinations my pet received (Photocopies are not acceptable).

☐ The vaccination certificates have the vaccine name, lot or serial number, booster interval, vaccination date and expiration date listed.

☐ I have an original health certificate in English, which was done within 14 days of arrival in Hawaii including rabies vaccine name, lot or serial number, booster interval, vaccination date and expiration date.

☐ My vet has treated my pet for ticks with a product containing Fipronil or an equivalent long-acting product (Revolution® is not acceptable) within 14 days of arrival and the product name and date of treatment is recorded on my health certificate.

☐ I have a copy of the Airport Release card given to me when my pet was released at the airport on a previous arrival in Hawaii if I am applying for re-entry under the same OIE-FAVN blood test and rabies vaccinations.

Step 6 SUBMISSION OF DOCUMENTS (Date Documents Were Sent:_____)
(Send documents and payment to: Animal Quarantine Station, 99-951 Halawa Valley Street, Aiea, Hawaii 96701.)

> **Note! Do not send each document in separately. Send all documents (Dog & Cat Import Form, two rabies vaccination certificates, etc) in as a set.** <u>**Faxes are not accepted!**</u>

☐ I have allowed necessary delivery time to ensure documentation is received by the Rabies Quarantine Branch **10 days or more before my pet is to arrive** in Hawaii for direct release.

☐ If I didn't send my original health certificate to the Rabies Quarantine Branch in advance of my pet's arrival when I submitted my other documents, I will provide the health certificate upon arrival at the Airport Animal Quarantine Holding Facility. If I fail to bring the original health certificate (photocopy not acceptable), my pet will not be released.

☐ Required Documentation:
(The Rabies Quarantine Branch must receive the following more than 10 days before my pet is scheduled to arrive in Hawaii!)

    ☐ My completed Pet Import Form AQS-278 (must be notarized).

    ☐ My 2 original rabies vaccination documents with original signature.

    ☐ I have paid my fees ($165 per pet in advance for direct airport release or $224 for 5-day-or-less program) by cashier's check or money order (no personal checks are accepted). I have included my pet's microchip number with my payment to ensure proper credit. Payable to: **Department of Agriculture.**

    ☐ My copy of the Airport Release card given to me when my pet was released at the airport on a previous arrival in Hawaii if I am applying as a re-entry under the same OIE-FAVN blood test and rabies vaccinations. (Be sure test and rabies vaccination is still valid!)

☐ I have sent my documents by mail with return receipt to verify delivery, or by another overnight carrier that provides tracking of my documents.

☐ I may still pay at the airport however, processing will be delayed. Payment by cashier's check or money order is recommended. VISA, MasterCard, traveler's checks and cash will also be accepted upon arrival, but may delay processing time. My payment will be made in full before my pet will be released. Payment in excess of fees will receive refunds through the mail in 6 to 8 weeks.

☐ I have copies of necessary qualification documents (health certificate, rabies vaccination records, and blood test result) for myself and to accompany my pet as a backup.

Step 7 OTHER

☐ I have verified my pet's qualification to participate in the 5-day-or-less program at the Hawaii Department of Agriculture web site: http://www.hawaiiag.org/hdoa/ai_aqs_info.htm

Direct Release at Airport

☐ I understand that Direct Release is only done at the **Honolulu International Airport.**

☐ I have arranged for my pet to arrive at the Airport Animal Quarantine Holding Facility at the Honolulu International Airport during normal inspection hours of 8:00 AM and 8:00 PM. I realize that it may usually take up to one hour for the airlines to transport my pet to the Airport Animal Quarantine Holding Facility [Phone: (808) 837-8092] and animals not arriving at the facility during normal inspection hours will not be released at the airport. Posted inspection hours are subject to change.

☐ I understand that animals on international flights will also need to clear U.S. Customs **before** they may be released from the Airport Animal Quarantine Holding Facility. Please check with your airlines regarding U.S. Customs hours of operation to assure they will be open to process your pet for release.

- ☐ If my pet is not picked up that day, it will be transferred to the Animal Quarantine Station at 8:30 AM the following morning and will be entered into the 5-day-or-less program. Fees for the 5-day-or-less program are $224 per pet.
- ☐ I understand my pet will not qualify for direct airport release if ticks or other parasites are found at the time of arrival.
- ☐ I understand that direct release at Honolulu International Airport will not be possible when prohibited by Federal airport security advisories. Under those circumstances pets will be released the following day at the Animal Quarantine Station 99-951 Halawa Valley Street, Aiea, Hawaii 96701, phone: (808) 483-7151, during normal office hours:

Monday through Friday:	9:00 AM to 11:00 AM & 1:00 PM to 4:30PM
Saturday, Sunday, State Holidays:	8:00 AM to 10:00 AM & 12:00 PM to 3:30PM

- ☐ I understand that an animal may only be released to the consignee identified on the shipmaster's declaration. If I am not traveling with my pet, I have made arrangements with the airlines to consign my pet to the individual who will pick up my pet.
- ☐ I understand that it is my responsibility to arrange all transportation for my pet once it is released from the Airport Animal Quarantine Holding Facility in Honolulu.

> NOTE! Pet owners should bring a baggage cart or other means to transport their crated pet from the Airport Animal Quarantine Holding Facility to the Inter-island Terminal if traveling on to an outer island after release of their pet. There are no carts or porters at the Airport Animal Quarantine Holding Facility.

- ☐ Due to Federal security regulations at the Honolulu International Airport, all pets that qualify for direct airport release must be secured in their flight carriers when picked up from the Airport Animal Quarantine Holding Facility until the animal is out of the Airport. **Do not remove your pet from its transport carrier on airport property!**
- ☐ I understand that I must notify the Animal Quarantine Station prior to arrival, follow the same procedures, and meet all the requirements each time my pet enters or returns to Hawaii.
- ☐ I understand that I will pay a fee of $165 per pet for direct airport release or $224 per pet for the 5-day-or-less program each time my pet enters or returns to Hawaii unless it qualifies for subsequent entry fees outlined in: "Re-Entry Fee Requirements".
- ☐ **5-Day-or-Less** - Pets arriving between 8:00 PM and 8:00 AM will be transferred to the Animal Quarantine Station and entered under the 5-day-or-less program. The first day of quarantine shall be the day following the date of animal arrival into the State. In this situation, after all necessary documents are received and verified, pets may be picked up at the Animal Quarantine Station, 99-951 Halawa Valley Street, Aiea, Hawaii 96701, phone: (808) 483-7151, during normal office hours:

Monday through Friday:	9:00 AM to 11:00 AM & 1:00 PM to 4:30 PM
Saturday, Sunday, State Holidays:	8:00 AM to 10:00 AM & 12:00 PM to 3:30 PM

- ☐ I understand that I will be assessed an additional $17.80 each day my pet remains at the Animal Quarantine Station beyond its scheduled release date. I will arrange to board my pet at a private facility after its release date.

Mexico

It is easy to cruise in Mexico. If you watch and listen to reports, the weather is simply delightful. Of course, never underestimate Mother Nature - use care and work your sail plan in harmony with nature. The Mexican people are her national treasure. The food is fantastic. I've eaten at little stands and neighborhood cafés all over the country and have only been ill... well... just a couple of times. Medical care (not veterinary care) is inexpensive, good and easy to come by. The scenery is varied and beautiful in every state and, should you get homesick, there's a cruiser or ex-pat just a short stroll away. Best of all, Kip McSnip was not only welcomed everywhere we traveled in Mexico – he was adored!

I'm a firm believer of spaying and neutering pets – for all the reasons you've heard a hundred times before. Kip had his surgery as soon as he was old enough, but I learned early on to always answer in the affirmative when Mexican men asked me if Kip was a "whole dog." When in Rome, at least chat like a Roman.

All you need to import your dog into Mexico is a current International Health Certificate stating that your pet has been vaccinated against rabies, hepatitis, pip and leptospirosis. I've read and heard that Mexico requires Health Certificates to be issued within 72 hours before arriving in the country. Other official sources indicate a 14-day grace period. We've cruised into Mexico several times and our experiences have been slightly different each time. I've only produced Kip's papers once. That time, my motley crew and I were sailing into Ensenada and got completely turned around trying to enter our marina. After several botched (and sloppy) turns, a group of fellows from the Mexican Navy came by to check us out. Who could blame them? We looked pretty disoriented. I led the group leader through an inspection of my boat while his men and my crew posed for snapshots in the cockpit. I showed him all my boat papers including Kip's papers. He pretended to examine them although it was pretty clear he didn't read English. We shook hands, posed for a photo and then he and his men helped us find the entrance to our marina. That was our most official encounter. In every other Mexican port I've simply presented my ship's papers and was clear. Kip has traveled all over that delightful country without mishap. Well, not very much mishap, at least.

I've included a story, *Life in a Mexican Barrio*, in the *Appendix* to illustrate how welcome both Kip and I felt while cruising in Mexico.

French Polynesia

The official rule about taking your dog ashore in French Polynesia is: You can't. However, according to several travel websites and phone conversations with representatives of the French Consulate, you can get special permission to take your dog ashore if you simply fax your request to the proper authorities in Tahiti. If your dog has been onboard your ship for a total of 28 days (and you can prove it using the check-out papers from your last port of call), and he has been micro-chipped and vaccinated, you will be granted an exception. This is great in theory. However, despite a month of phone calls (one of my friends speaks fluent French and did most of the talking for me) and several faxes and certified letters, we were never able to get a reply from the officials in Tahiti. We had a personal name and direct phone and fax line number of the gentleman in charge but the fellow simply refused to acknowledge any of our requests. Eventually, it came time for me to weigh anchor and head out. I covered all my bases by going through all the proper check-out procedures in Mexico, by making sure Kip had every possible vaccine, and by securing multiple copies of all the official documents and certifications I could lay my hands on. Our weather window opened and we couldn't wait any longer. So, hoping for the best, we set sail for French Polynesia.

A shimmery copper light painted the dark leaves of banana trees rimming the shoreline. My crew member, Mike Irvine, and I sat on the deck of *Blessed Be!* inhaling our first scent of land in twenty-five days. We'd just dropped the hook after crossing the Pacific. Eigteen hours earlier we had lost our steering, seen our dinghy escape to sea and became dismasted. We'd fought against the trade winds, almost crashed into a rocky shoreline and now, finally, we'd managed to limp into a quiet cove on the north side of Hiva Oa. The boat looked like a floating pile of bomb debris but we were alive. Kip wandered around on deck sniffing at torn sails and twisted rigging.

"Look," Mike shielded his eyes against the brilliant setting sun and pointed to the mouth of the bay. A dark-skinned man covered with traditional tattoos paddled a plastic kayak across the water. We were beside ourselves with excitement when we learned the man spoke English. His name was Eric and he asked us what we were doing there. We told him about the crossing and, gesturing toward the wreckage, we described being dismasted.

"You are the first person we've seen in almost a month," we said." Can you help us find a way to get to shore?" Eric listened to our story and then gave us this advice:

"You have to declare the dog. You must go immediately to the gendarmes [local police] and tell them you have a dog. You cannot take that animal to the shore." Mike and I weren't sure we'd been clear. We repeated our story: Emergency at sea. Forced to land. No way to get even ourselves to shore. No way to move our boat. Eric listened. Then he demanded that we turn Kip in immediately. "You must report that animal now!" he declared. Then, he calmly paddled away.

When I finally did make it to the gendarme's office in Atuona I declared Kip on an official document. However, the police were much more concerned about the safety of my crew and the well-being of the boat than with an 18-year-old dog potentially taking a stroll on a deserted path. For the next week, I was so busy jury-rigging my boat enough to sail it to Tahiti (for proper repairs), I didn't have time to even think of sneaking Kip ashore. Kip didn't seem to care a bit. He was quite content to stay onboard.

We reached the Tuamotoes in six days. Again, I declared Kip on an official document, but the gendarmes on Rangiroa had never seen that particular form, and, after giving it a quick glance, they returned it to me. They were interested in how much horsepower my Perkins 4108 diesel engine had. I asked them about bringing Kip ashore and they just looked at each other and shrugged. It didn't seem to matter one way or the other. Again, this was simply my experience at the time. The written law is very clear. How closely local officials subscribe to the law may vary from island to island and maybe even from week to week. We stayed anchored in front of an upscale resort for a week and then moved on to Raiatea.

Because my boat repairs took longer than expected, we ended up spending several weeks on the island of Raiatea. Although it was a definite detour in my cruising itinerary, the time spent with the folks on that pristine island will always be a jewel among my memories. Kip and I used our time getting to know the island, her people, and the fresh fruits and fragrant floral bouquets that characterize Raiatea. I declared Kip in the official paperwork and asked if he could come ashore. Again, the answer was simply a shrug. No one seemed to care one way or the other if Kip and I took an evening stroll through the boatyard or along the peaceful stretch of road flanking the beach.

Australia

Australia has strict rules about the importation of animals; however, the rules are clear and easy to follow. Quarantine requirements vary depending on where you've been traveling and your pet's country of origin. Even with friendly people and easy to follow regulations, you can see from the Fall 2006 announcement posted by the Australian government, getting your pet into Australia can be difficult.

AVAILABILITY OF SPACE FOR CATS AND DOGS AT ANIMAL QUARANTINE STATIONS

The Australian Quarantine and Inspection Service (AQIS) wishes to advise that all Australian animal quarantine stations are at full capacity and all stations are fully booked for several months. People wishing to have their pets accommodated at an Australian animal quarantine station should apply for an import permit at least 5 months in advance of anticipated departure. An import permit does not guarantee a space at an animal quarantine station.

BOOKINGS MUST BE MADE FOR YOUR PET(S).

To book a space at an Australian animal quarantine station, a permit number is required. Once an import permit has been issued for your pet(s) and you have a permit number, contact the relevant animal quarantine station to make a reservation. **Please note the waiting time can be at least 5 months.** Provision of an airway bill number to the animal quarantine station will be required to confirm your pet(s) reservation closer to the time of departure.

The following information was compiled by ChinaRoad Lochens of Australia. As of January 2007, the information is current; however, the laws around international travel (for pets and for people) change regularly. I suggest you check this website periodically www.lowchensqustralia.com/quaratine. ChinaRoad Lochens does a superior job of updating their site as the rules change.

Guide to importing pets into Australia from approved countries (by category)

Category 1
No quarantine in Australia

New Zealand

Category 2
30 days quarantine in Australia

Bahrain, Barbados, Cyprus, Falkland Islands, Fiji, French Polynesia (includes Tahiti, Society Islands, Marquesas Islands, Austral Islands, Tuamotu Islands, Gambier Islands), Guam, Hawaii, the Republic of Ireland, Japan, Malta, Mauritius, New Caledonia, Norway, Singapore, Sweden, Taiwan, the United Kingdom, Vanuatu.

Category 3A
60 days quarantine in Australia

American Samoa, Cook Islands, Federated States of Micronesia, Kiribati, Papua New Guinea, Solomon Islands, Kingdom of Tonga, Wallis and Futuna, Western Samoa.

Category 3B
60 days quarantine in Australia

Christmas Island, Nauru, Niue, Palau, Tuvalu.

Category 4
Minimum 30 days quarantine in Australia

Antigua and Barbuda, Austria, Bahamas, Belgium, Bermuda, British Virgin Islands, Brunei, Canada, Cayman Islands, Chile, Croatia, Czech Republic, Denmark, France, Finland, Germany, Greece, Greenland, Hong Kong, Hungary, Israel, Italy, Jamaica, Kuwait, Luxembourg, Macau, Peninsular Malaysia, Netherlands, Netherlands Antilles and Aruba, Portugal, Puerto Rico, Qatar, Reunion, Sabah, Sarawak, Seychelles, Slovenia Republic, South Korea, Spain, St. Kitts and Nevis, St. Lucia, St.Vincent Grenadin, Saipan, Switzerland (including Liechtenstein), Trinidad and Tobago, United Arab Emirates, United States of America, US Virgin Islands, Uruguay, Yugoslavia Republic (including Montenegro, Serbia and Kosovo).

Category 5
120 days quarantine in Australia

Republic of South Africa

Category 6

All other countries - Australian Offshore Territories
No quarantine in Australia, Cocos (Keeling) Islands, Norfolk Island

• • •

You can download specific rules for each category by going to www.lowchensqustralia.com/quarantine

DIAGNOSTIC TESTING FOR IMPORTING/EXPORTING CATS AND DOGS

For cats or dogs to be imported into or exported from Australia, they must be shown to be free from disease. This capability outlines procedures for submitting blood samples from your cat or dog for testing at CSIRO's Australian Animal Health Laboratory (AAHL).

111

Tests undertaken at the Australian Animal Health Laboratory (AAHL)

CSIRO's Australian Animal Health Laboratory can undertake the following tests (subject to minimum testing fee):

Serological Test	Dogs	Cats	Cost in $AUD where GST does not apply	Cost in $AUD where GST applies
Rabies virus neutralization test (RFFIT)*	YES	YES	$109.09	$120.00
Nipah virus serum neutralization test (SNT)	YES	YES	$175.00	$192.50
Nipah virus enzyme-linked immunosorbent assay (ELISA)	YES	YES	$54.54	$60.00
Brucella canis tube serum agglutination test (SAT)	YES	NO	$54.54	$60.00
Ehrlicha canis immuno-flourescent antibody test (IFAT)	YES	NO	$127.27 (first test) $63.64 each additional test if you have more than one dog tested at the same time	$140.00 (first test) $70.00 each additional test if you have more than one dog tested at the same time
Leptospira canicola microscopic agglutination test (MAT)	YES	NO	$75.00	$82.50
Hendra virus serum neutralization test (SNT)	YES	YES	$75.00	$82.50
Hendra virus enzyme-linked immunosorbent assay (ELISA)	YES	YES	$54.54	$60.00
Minimum testing charge			$90.91	$100.00
TOTAL				

AAHL Accessions Administrators
CSIRO Australian Animal Health Laboratory (AAHL)
5 Portarlington Road
EAST GEELONG VIC AUSTRALIA 3219
Fax: +613 5227 5555

AQIS Animal Quarantine Offices

New South Wales 2 Hayes Rd,
Rosebery, Sydney (02) 9364 7396
8:00 a.m. to 11:00 a.m.

Victoria Quarantine House, Landside Road,
Tullamarine, Melbourne (03) 9338 3344
8:30 a.m. to 11:45 a.m.

Tasmania Mt. Pleasant Laboratories,
Dept. of Primary Energy & Fisheries
Kings Meadows (03) 6336 5334
By prior arrangement

North Queensland Airport Administration Centre
Cairns International Airport, Cairns (07) 4030 7800
By prior arrangement

Queensland Qantas Drive
Eagle Farm, Brisbane (07) 3246 8731
8:30 a.m. to 12 noon

South Australia 8 Butler Street
Port Adelaide (08) 8305 9752
2:00 p.m.

Western Australia Market Square
280 Bannister Rd (Center Ranford Rd),
Canning Vale (08) 9311 5333
10:30 a.m. to 12 noon.

Northern Territory John England Building, Berrimah Farm, Makagon Road, Berrimah. NT 0828 (08) 8999 2093 8:00 a.m. to 4:20 p.m.

Australian Capital Territory Edmund Barton Building, Blackall Street, Barton ACT (02) 6272 4581 11:00 a.m. to 12 noon 2:30 p.m. to 4.30 p.m.

You can visit and interact with your pet during its stay in quarantine. Because visiting hours differ between stations, please refer to the stations below for details.

Eastern Creek Quarantine Station
Sydney, New South Wales 60 Wallgrove Rd
Eastern Creek, NSW 2766
Phone: 61 (0)2 9625 4566
Fax: 61 (0)2 9832 1532
EasternCreek.AQS@aqis.gov.au

Spotswood Animal Quarantine Station
Victoria43-47 Craig St
Spotswood,Victoria 3015
Phone: 61 3 9391 1627
Fax: 61 3 9391 0860
SpotswoodQuarantine@aqis.gov.au

Byford Quarantine Station
Western Australia Nettleton Road
Byford WA 6122
Phone: 61 8 9525 1763
Fax: 61 8 9526 2199
BYFORDQ@aqis.gov.au

APPLICATION FORM FOR A PERMIT TO IMPORT CATS AND DOGS INTO AUSTRALIA

The most current information including approved country lists can be obtained via the Internet at **www.aqis.gov.au** or by e-mail at **animalimp@aqis.gov.au** or by ph +612 6272 4454.

- You must complete one application for each cat or dog. Note: This application is not an import permit.
- The completed application form/s should be posted or faxed to the quarantine station that will accommodate your pet/s on arrival in Australia (stations are listed on the last page of this application).
- A sum of AUD **$260** must be sent with the application/s. This fee is payable only once per owner when multiple pets arrive in Australia at the same time. If sending a cheque, your application should be posted, if paying by credit card you may post or fax your application. Cheques are payable to the "Collector of Public Monies-AQIS" - Amex, Visa, Matercard and Bankcard are accepted.
- AQIS will send an import permit/s (including veterinary certificates A and B) to you after receiving the completed application/s. Pets are only eligible to travel to Australia with a valid AQIS import permit and when all conditions provided on the AQIS import permit have been met.
- The owner/importer must pay all **quarantine fees** associated with the import and quarantine accommodation of pet/s.

SECTIONS 1, 2, 3, 4 and **5** must be completed by all applicants.
SECTION 6 should only be completed if importing more than one animal.
SECTION 7 must be completed if importing a dog from a country where dog-mediated rabies is absent or well controlled ie category 4 or South Africa. An OFFICIAL VETERINARIAN of the country of export must complete this section. There is no need to fill out section 7 if you are importing a cat or dog from a rabies free country ie category 2 or 3.

---

1. Country of origin

The country of origin of your cat or dog:...

Approximate date of export:...

---

2. Importer details

Details of IMPORTER /Owner or Representative in Australia:

Mr/Mrs/Ms:...................................(surname)...................................(given name)

Address:...

....Postcode................

....AUSTRALIA.   E-mail...

Telephone:(Home)...............................(Work) ....Fax:............................

---

3. Exporter details

Details of the EXPORTER / owner / representative in the country of origin:

Mr/ Mrs/ Ms:...(surname)...(given name)

Address:...

....Postcode...........

....E-mail:..

Telephone:(Home)...............................(Work) .... Fax:...............................
Please include country codes and area codes.

Please either type or write clearly in BLOCK letters. Where applicable, please tick the relevant box ☑.

4. Description of animal	
Animal's name:	Age or date of birth(day/month/year): ....
Species: Dog ☐ Cat ☐	Sex: Male (entire) ☐ Male de-sexed ☐ Female (entire) ☐ Female de-sexed ☐
Breed (for mixed breed animals, indicate the breed/s which the animal most closely resembles): .... Pregnancy: Will the animal be pregnant on arrival in Australia? No ☐ Yes ☐ Expected date of birth (day/month/year)...	

5. Microchip details AQIS can not issue a permit to import if this section is not completed.	
Microchip number:	Microchip reader type: Avid ☐ Destron ☐ Trovan ☐ Other ISO Compatible:.........................

6. Animals sharing quarantine accommodation. Please complete this section if you are intending to import more than one animal. Shared accommodation will only be granted for animals of the same species.

Do you want this cat/dog to share quarantine accommodation with another pet owned by you?

No ☐

Yes ☐ Name, microchip number and species of other animal: ....

....

DECLARATION

I declare that this animal is not a Pitbull Terrier or American Pitbull Terrier or Fila Brasileiro or Dogo Argentino or Japanese Tosa. Also, the animal is not a domestic animal hybrid such as a wolf or bengal cat having any pure-bred ancestor less than 5th generations away.

I declare that to the best of my knowledge and belief all the above information is true and correct

....
(Signature and printed name of applicant)   Date:..........................

116

7. Rabies vaccination and Rabies Neutralising Antibody Titre Testing (RNATT).
This section must completed when importing animals from a category 4 country or South Africa.

THIS SECTION MUST BE COMPLETED, SIGNED AND STAMPED BY AN OFFICIAL VETERINARIAN OF THE COUNTRY OF EXPORT. A PERMIT TO IMPORT WILL NOT BE ISSUED IF ANY PART OF THIS SECTION IS BLANK. [A copy of the RNATT must be attached]

I ....(Name of Official Veterinarian)

....…......(Address of Official Veterinarian)

declare that I have sighted the rabies vaccination certificate and the RNATT report.

• The date of last rabies vaccination is recorded as: ....

• The animals age at last rabies vaccination was:..…...........

• The laboratory reporting the RNATT is government-approved: Yes ☐
• Name and address of approved laboratory:..

....

• The microchip number that appears on the RNATT report is:...

• Blood samples taken for RNATT were drawn on:........................…...................…......(dd/mm/yy)

• The RNATT result is recorded as:............….....................…......International Units/ml in animal's serum

(the RNATT result must be at least 0.5IU/ml)

....
Signature of Official Veterinarian   **Stamp of Official Veterinarian**

Faxed applications must bear the stamp of the Official Veterinarian rather than a raised seal.

AQIS Animal Quarantine Sydney - New South Wales	AQIS Animal Quarantine Melbourne - Victoria -	AQIS Animal Quarantine Perth - Western Australia
Eastern Creek Animal Quarantine Station 60 Wallgrove Rd Eastern Creek NSW 2766	Spotswood Animal Quarantine Station PO Box 300 Newport VIC 3015	Byford Animal Quarantine Station PO Box 61 Byford WA 6201
Fax: (612) 9832 1532	Fax: (613) 9391 0860	Fax: (618) 9526 2199

Additional Regulations for Dogs Arriving on Private Yachts

A quarantine officer will inspect your vessel when you arrive at your proclaimed first ports of entry in Australia. During the inspection of your vessel, a quarantine officer will inspect your ship's pet and, provided the animal is showing no signs of an infectious disease (e.g. Rabies, Newcastle Disease, etc), the animal may stay onboard your vessel while in Australian ports or waters. The quarantine officer will explain to you the quarantine requirements for the safe keeping of your pet while in Australia (also given to you in writing) and, provided all quarantine conditions are met by you during your stay (e.g. not taking the animal ashore under any circumstances, unless you have permission from a quarantine officer), you should have no problems meeting the quarantine conditions while in Australia.

All international yachts carrying animal(s) onboard **must** go to a mid-water anchorage on arrival at your proclaimed first port of call in Australia (see the Australian Quarantine and Inspection Service – AQIS – website for the list of Australian proclaimed ports). When a quarantine officer attends your vessel, you will be called into the quarantine boarding station where formal quarantine inspection and clearance will be conducted. All vessels with animal(s) onboard will be given written directions for the control, confinement and prevention of escape of the animal(s) from the vessel, and the site for mooring or berthing the vessel while in Australian ports or waters.

If you intend to change moorings, you must advise AQIS of your intention to move your vessel from its current moorings at least 48 hours prior to any movement of the vessel. A proposed itinerary of the vessel's movements in Australian ports or waters must be provided to AQIS, and any changes to the proposed itinerary must also be brought to the attention of AQIS.

It is important that all animal(s) be confined and controlled at all times while the vessel is in Australian ports or waters. The control and confinement of the animal(s) is most important during cyclonic conditions or other emergency situations, or in other circumstances as advised by AQIS (i.e. when the vessel is left unattended). All animal waste must be disposed of in a manner approved by AQIS. These arrangements may change on a port-by-port basis. Therefore, you are advised to check with the local port quarantine officer in relation to port quarantine requirements.

All dogs and/or cats onboard the vessel **must** be confined in a manner consistent with the written directions provided by AQIS at all times. The general conditions for the safe keeping of dogs and cats onboard international yachts while in Australian ports or waters include:

Placed on a tether and locked below decks, when the owners are away from the vessel.

Must not be taken ashore for exercise by their owners.

Must not be taken ashore, without the permission of AQIS.

The master will ensure all animal waste is disposed of in a manner approved by AQIS.

The owner will be responsible for all AQIS fees and charges relating to the retention of dogs or cats onboard the vessel, which may include quarantine surveillance, if non-compliance with quarantine requirements is detected during the vessels stay in Australian ports or waters.

Please Note: The AQIS requirements for the control and confinement for dogs and cats only applies to animals onboard foreign registered overseas vessels. Returning Australian registered vessels, with dogs or cats onboard will require the removal of the animal(s) from the vessel for the required mandatory period of quarantine, to be served in a quarantine station at the owner's expense. It is recommended that the mandatory period of quarantine should be undertaken as soon as possible if the animal(s) are to remain permanently in Australia.

All animals imported into Australia require a 'Permit To Import Quarantine Material' issued by AQIS. Applications to import dogs and cats brought into Australia on international yachts are assessed on a case-by-case basis. All dogs and cats, except those imported directly from New Zealand, will spend a minimum of 30 days in quarantine at a Government Quarantine Station. The exact period of quarantine confinement will be determined by the countries that have been visited in the previous six months and the testing performed previously on the animal.

Countries are assigned a disease risk category based on an assessment of the overall disease status of the country concerned. In order to qualify for the minimum of 30 days quarantine, it is recommended that in the six months prior to import, you visit only the following countries (Category 1 and 2): New Zealand, Norfolk Island, Fiji, French Polynesia (includes Tahiti), Guam, Hawaii, Vanuatu and New Caledonia.

If countries from categories 3, 4, 5 and 6 have been visited in the preceding six months the period of quarantine will be determined by countries visited, rabies vaccination status and test results from a Rabies Antibody Neutralising Antibody Titre Test (RNATT). The dogs and cats will be imported according to the import conditions in respect of the country that has the highest category grade that has been visited.

Documentary evidence must be provided to support stated ports of call in the previous six months (e.g. ship's log, passports, Customs/ quarantine certificates of clearance and/or admission endorsed by the relevant port authority where possible). If supporting documentation is found to be inadequate, a longer period of quarantine may be imposed.

If a non-approved country has been visited in the last six months, the animals will be required to serve a quarantine period of six months, since departing the non-approved country.

International yachts arriving with animals onboard intended for importation **must** proceed immediately to an AQIS controlled port. The AQIS preferred position is to have animals requiring post arrival quarantine to enter at the port closest to a quarantine facility. You will be required to proceed to a mid-water anchorage on arrival and notify AQIS. A quarantine officer will attend your vessel and you will be called into the quarantine boarding station, where your pet will be sealed into its cage. Arrangements must be made for movement of the animal(s) from the vessel to the quarantine facility under AQIS control. All costs associated with transportation from the vessel to the quarantine station will be at the importer's expense.

All dogs and cats imported into Australia onboard international yachts will be tested during Post Arrival Quarantine (PAQ) in Australia for Leptospira Canicola, Brucella Canis and Ehrlichia Canis at the owner's expense and will not be eligible for release from quarantine until they fully comply with the relevant import permit conditions.

AQIS regulates the quarantine requirements for animals entering Australian ports and waters and the Department of the Environment (DEH) regulates the import and export of wildlife in Australia. Therefore, if you intend to bring a pet on your vessel into Australian waters, in addition to complying with the AQIS requirements, you must contact DEH to determine if there are any further import requirements. For further information, please refer to the DEH website or send your email enquiry to wsm@deh.gov.au.

(Almost) everywhere else

The following list of rules regarding the importation of domestic pets is a distillation of information found on numerous websites. These websites are listed in <u>Resources</u>. This list is simply an overview. Be sure to check out each country's website and if possible, talk with cruisers in the area to learn the most up-to-date information.

<u>American Samoa:</u> In addition to posting a bond of $500 (U.S. currency), your pet will be quarantined on your boat.

<u>Anguilla:</u> Use caution and be very deliberate in your preparations due to strict regulations/policies and/or long quarantines.

<u>Antigua:</u> Use caution and be very deliberate in your preparations due to strict regulations/policies and/or long quarantines (six months) – unless your pet is from an approved quarantine area.

<u>Aruba:</u> Pets from Central and South America are not permitted. Dogs and cats are permitted with the presentation of a veterinary certified Health Certificate and rabies vaccination.

<u>Bahamas:</u> For all pets you must present an import permit from the Ministry of Agriculture, Trade and Industry. Among other things, this permit certifies that dogs and cats from the U.S./Canada are at least six months old, have been vaccinated against rabies within the past ten months but not more recently than one month, and have been examined by a vet within 48 hours of arrival along with the pet's Health Certificate.

<u>Barbados:</u> Use caution and be very deliberate in your preparations due to strict regulations/policies and/or long quarantines.

<u>Belize:</u> You must present a valid Health Certificate issued not more than 48 hours from the time of departure as well as verification of rabies vaccination within the previous six months but not more

recently than one month. Dogs must also be certifiably vaccinated against distemper, infectious canine hepatitis, leptospirosis, and parvovirus. Re-vaccination will be required if your documents are considered insufficient. Finally, you'll need to obtain an import permit from a vet in Belize.

Bermuda: You must present the requisite import permit for your pet.

Bonaire: Pets are permitted with valid Health Certificate and rabies vaccination.

Brazil: Dogs, cats, and birds are allowed with a certified rabies vaccination, a vet-authorized sanitary certificate (approved by Veterinary Services and legalized at a Brazilian Consulate) dated within one week of departure. The sanitary certificate must also verify that no contagious diseases were detected in your pet's place of origin within 40 days of departure. All certified documents must also be verified by the Consular Service. Other animals must be approved prior to arrival by the Ministry of Agriculture.

British Virgin Islands: You must abide by the same rules that govern admission to the United Kingdom, which is governed by the regulations of the Pet Travel Scheme.

Caicos Islands: In addition to having your pet examined by a public health inspector upon arrival, you must present a veterinary certified Health Certificate and rabies vaccination.

Cayman Islands: In addition to the required import permit/animal passport issued by the Cayman Islands and associated fee, you must present an Official Health Certificate that was issued within 14 days of your arrival. Certain breeds are prohibited, as are cats and dogs from Asia, Africa, Central and South America, Cuba, Puerto Rico, Haiti and the Dominican Republic.

China: Use caution and be very deliberate in your preparations due to strict regulations/policies and/or long quarantines.

Costa Rica: If applicable, you need to provide proof of your payment of the appropriate Customs duty. You also need an invoice or other proof of your pet's market value, a quarantine permit from the Ministry of Agriculture and Animal Control in Costa Rica, and a certified Health Certificate additionally verified by a Veterinary Services (VS) veterinarian at the U. S. Department of Agriculture Animal and Plant Health Inspection Service.

Curacao: You must present a valid Health Certificate.

Denmark: For dogs and cats older than three months you must provide veterinary Health Certificates and documentation of rabies vaccination within one year but not more recently than one month. Dogs and cats younger than three months do not require rabies vaccination if you provide a veterinary certificate confirming that no outbreak of rabies has occurred within 20 kilometers of the animal's area of origin within 60 days of departure.

Dominican Republic: Make sure that the required certified Health Certificate (issued after examination within 30 days of departure) contains complete contact information for you, the owner, and complete identification of your pet. A certified rabies vaccination should have been administered and documented no more than one year prior to arrival and no less than one month.

Dominica: You must present a certified Health Certificate and the appropriate import permit from the Veterinary Officer of the Ministry of Agriculture in the Commonwealth of Dominica.

Ecuador: Your certified Health Certificate must verify vaccination within 60 days of departure against the following: panleucopenia (cats), distemper, hepatitis, leptospirosis, parvovirosis, rabies, influenza, and parasites (more than thirty days before departure). It must also verify normal health and the lack of tumors, wounds, quarantined transferable diseases, and the presence of ectoparasites. Special cages and boxes are required for shipping, the authentication of which includes a consular fee of $50 (U.S. currency).

Egypt: Dogs and cats must have a certified Health Certificate but will still be examined upon arrival. Pets will be quarantined, for no longer than 15 days, if disease is suspected.

Fiji: Dogs and cats may be imported into Fiji only from Australia, Canada, New Zealand, United Kingdom, and United States (including Hawaii). Pets from all other countries must first be exported to one of the listed countries and meet their quarantine regulations before potentially being exported to Fiji. Pets arriving in yachts must stay aboard for the entire duration of your stay.

Finland: You must present a certified Health Certificate that was issued within ten days of your arrival (that must verify clearance of any internal parasites). You must also provide documentation of vaccination against rabies and distemper no more than one year ago and no less than one month.

France: A certified Health Certificate dated within five days of arrival/departure is recommended but not required. However, you must provide documentation of rabies vaccination within 12 months of arrival but not more recently than one month.

Germany: You must provide certified documentation of your pet's good health and vaccination against rabies within 12 months of arrival.

Greece: Your certified Health Certificate (issued within 10 days of departure) must verify no symptoms of infectious/contagious disease, rabies vaccination within twelve months but not less than 15 days, and treatment against echinococcosis within 30 days of departure. Birds must be certified to be free of psittacosis.

<u>Grenada:</u> Pets without an import permit are prohibited. The Government Veterinary Officer must be notified prior to your arrival, and the necessary documents must be produced.

<u>Guadeloupe:</u> Dogs and cats over three months of age are permitted with a certificate of origin and a certified Health Certificate or documentation of rabies vaccination.

<u>Ireland:</u> Use caution and be very deliberate in your preparations due to strict regulations/policies and/or long quarantines.

<u>Israel:</u> Dogs and cats younger than three months are not permitted. For other pets not considered wildlife, a veterinary import permit is not required provided you have a certified Health Certificate issued within seven days of your departure (including a declaration that you have been in possession of your pet for the previous 90 days) and an international rabies vaccination certificate verifying inoculation at least one month prior but not more than 12 months. In order to avoid quarantine (which varies), you must notify the Ramla Quarantine Station 48 hours prior to your arrival that you are bringing a pet/pets.

<u>Italy:</u> Pets in good health, with rabies vaccination, are permitted.

<u>Jamaica:</u> Pets are not allowed due to rabies.

<u>Japan:</u> Dogs and cats are permitted after a quarantine time of 14 days. You must also present a certified Health Certificate and documentation of rabies vaccination within 12 months of arrival but not more recently than one month.

<u>Martinique:</u> Dogs and cats over three months of age are permitted with a certificate of origin and a certified Health Certificate or documentation of rabies vaccination.

<u>Montserrat:</u> Pets will be quarantined between three and six months. You must also present a certified Health Certificate and documentation of vaccination.

<u>New Caledonia:</u> Pets will be quarantined – *only* if you want to take them ashore – for ten days.

<u>New Zealand:</u> A quarantine clearance can only be sought for pets arriving from specific countries and must be approved by the Chief Veterinary Officer (who will also decide, if quarantine is needed, the necessary length of time). You must apply for an import permit in advance of your arrival, and you must also have the following forms: Veterinary Certificate A and Importer's Declaration. Your pet must also be properly identified and be accompanied by the corresponding certification. The New Zealand Ministry of Agriculture and Forestry must be notified of your arrival and that you have a pet before you get to one of the following ports: Opua, Whangerei, Auckland, Tauranga, Gisborne, New Plymouth, Hastings, Wellington, Nelson, Christchurch, Dunedin or Invercargill.

<u>Panama:</u> Landing is not permitted for travelers with pets.

<u>Puerto Rico:</u> As a United States territory, you need only present a certified Health Certificate and verification of vaccinations.

<u>Punta Cana:</u> You must provide a rabies vaccination certificate verifying that immunization was administered *at least* 30 days prior and a health certificate *not more than* 15 days old (from the time you arrive). Otherwise, length of quarantine varies from 8 to 30 days, according to country of origin.

<u>Singapore:</u> All pets not originating from Australia, New Zealand, the United Kingdom or Ireland must be quarantined for 30 days. Certain breeds are restricted entirely. Be sure, as with any country, that you investigate the policies surrounding quarantine before your departure.

<u>St. Barts:</u> Dogs and cats over three months of age are permitted with a certificate of origin and a certified Health Certificate or documentation of rabies vaccination.

<u>St. Kitts/Nevis:</u> Use caution and be very deliberate in your preparations due to strict regulations/policies and/or long quarantines.

<u>St. Lucia:</u> Use caution and be very deliberate in your preparations due to strict regulations/policies and/or long quarantines.

<u>St. Martin:</u> You must present a certified Health Certificate issued within 10 days of departure and a rabies vaccination certificate issued no more than 12 months prior to arrival and not less than one month.

<u>St. Vincent:</u> Pets from the United Kingdom, New Zealand, and Australia who have a certified Health Certificate are permitted. Pets from other countries must be quarantined for six months. Pets are allowed in Vincentian waters on yachts but must meet the above regulations to travel ashore.

<u>Switzerland:</u> You must provide a rabies vaccination certificate verifying that immunization was administered *at least* 30 days prior to arrival but *not more than* a year previously.

<u>Tonga:</u> In addition to a valid Health Certificate and rabies vaccination certificate, you must have an import permit for your pet.

<u>Trinidad:</u> Pets are not permitted to land.

<u>Tuvalu:</u> In addition to a valid Health Certificate and rabies vaccination certificate, you must have an import permit for your pet.

<u>United Kingdom:</u> Your pet(s) must be cleared for arrival according to the regulations of the Pet Travel Scheme, which includes the following procedures that must be carried out in order: Micro-chip-

ping, vaccination, blood test, PETS certificate, ticks and tapeworm treatment, declaration of residency.

<u>U.S. Virgin Islands:</u> You must provide a certified Health Certificate.

<u>Vanuatu:</u> Pets are not permitted to land.

<u>Venezuela:</u> Landing is permitted.

<u>Western Samoa:</u> After receiving a rabies vaccination, your pet must be quarantined for 120 days.

What documents do I need to carry for my dog?

You can save yourself a great deal of hassle by making multiple copies of all of your dog's health records (go back to the first inoculation if you can). Also, make several (a dozen would be perfect) copies of his International Health Certificate. I also make photocopies of his rabies tags even though the paper documents include the same information as the tags. Make copies of his micro-chipping records – the official numbers as well all the contact information. If your dog is registered with the American Kennel Club (AKC), or any other official organization, make several copies of the registration papers. Take a couple good, clear photos of your pet (from the side and the front) and make several copies of each. These "mutt mug shots" may help for identification purposes later. In any case, they will show how thorough you are. Leave your original copies on land - either in your safety deposit box or with the person who handles your bills and correspondence while you're out cruising. If you need more copies later, you'll be happy your originals are safe and dry.

The next step is to stamp each document (the copies, not the originals) with your ship's stamp. If you don't have a ship's stamp yet, take the time to create one. You'll need it for many documents as you cruise. You can design and order a ship's stamp at any large office supply store such as Staples, Office Max and Office Depot. Copy centers such as FedEx Kinko's usually make custom stamps as well. And, of course, you can order almost anything online. My ship's stamp is round and looks a great deal like an old-fashioned notary stamp. The outer ring has the name of my vessel and her U.S. Coast Guard Documentation number. The symbol I've designed for my boat's logo fills the center of a circle. Most copy centers have several standard clip art logos (of powerboats, sailboats, anchors, the compass rose, etc.) to choose from if you don't have your own. I use a red inked stamp pad because it looks so official. I stamp every document that goes into my ship's papers. Why? As you're cruising you'll gather a great deal of "official" paperwork and the officials issuing this paperwork will do a lot of "stamping." I've found that if I stamp next to their stamp, everything and everyone, seems more official. It seems to validate the work of the Customs officials - especially those in remote areas. They take their work very seriously. Be respectful as you stamp documents; you'll show your respect for their positions and you'll emphasize your own important position as ship's captain. Stamp your pet's papers to give them an official look as well.

After you've stamped your copies, put one set in your Ditch Bag and another set with your ship's papers. Laminate your documents or store them in waterproof document carriers. At the very least, double bag them in Ziploc baggies. Several trips into shore in your dinghy can be pretty rough on paperwork.

Be sure to carry your dog's papers along with the rest of your ship and crew papers when you check in with customs and immigrations officials. Always - ALWAYS - declare your pet. Even in areas where your pet will not be allowed off your vessel you must tell Customs officials you have a dog onboard. Failing to do so can be viewed as a sort of "hiding the evidence," and you run the risk of being told to leave the area, pay a large fine, or worse - your pet may be killed. Some countries will ask you to complete a Customs Declaration Form listing what you have onboard. They'll ask you to list electronic equipment, firearms, medicines and so forth. This is another place you'll want to list your pet.

These are the basic papers you'll need; however, you'll probably collect a stack of additional forms and documents along the way.

Before writing this I looked at the file I'd collected when returning from a trip with Kip. In addition to the papers we normally carry, I'd collected eleven new "official documents" before we finally cleared Customs, and there were three more government forms to be com-

pleted, paid for and stamped once we landed in Los Angeles.

Now, it is possible that you'll have all your papers in perfect order and the agent in charge of Customs and Immigration may not even glance at them. But being organized and prepared can only help smooth your experience moving through the official paper chase.

RESOURCES

Travel Crates

CONTAINER REQUIREMENT 1

The illustrations shown in this Container Requirement are examples only. Containers that conform to the principle of written guidelines for the species but look slightly different will still meet the IATA standards.

Applicable to:

Cats (domestic)

Dogs (domestic)

STATE VARIATIONS: CHG-01/03/04, GBG-01/02/03/04/05, HKG-01, NZG-01, SAG-02, ZVG-02/03/04, EUR-01, USG Variations

OPERATOR VARIATIONS: AF-01, BA-04/05, AC-03, CO-04/05/06/07/08/09/10, EI-01, EK-05, LX-05/06, OK-01/05, SV-01, QF-01

Note:
For carriage of domestic pets in passenger cabins as accompanied baggage see Chapters 2 and 3.

1. CONTAINER CONSTRUCTION

(Some governmental regulations require that the container must be sealed during transportation. Certain airlines will not carry wooden containers. See exceptions AUG-01 and NZG-01 in Chapter 2; AC-01 and QF-01 in Chapter 3.)

Materials

Fibreglass, metal, rigid plastics, weld metal mesh, solid wood or plywood.

Principles of Design

The following principles of design must be met in addition to the General Container Requirements outlined at the beginning of this chapter.

Containers made entirely of welded mesh or wire mesh are not suitable for air transport.

Rigid plastic containers are suitable for most breeds of dog but their acceptability is at the discretion of the carrier. If a container has wheels, they must be removed or rendered inoperable.

Some rigid plastic containers may not be suitable for large dogs, or dogs that are aggressive. Specially constructed containers of hardwood, metal, plywood or similar material, with two secure door fasteners on each side, are acceptable.

Size

Each animal contained in the container must have enough space to turn about normally while standing, to stand and sit erect, and to lie in a natural position.

Frame

For wooden containers, an outer frame of 2.5 cm × 7.5 cm (1 inch × 3 inch) lumber screwed or bolted together and lined with solid wood or plywood sides is acceptable.

Sides

For two part, rigid plastic containers, all hardware must be present and properly installed. Plywood of a minimum of 12 mm (1/2 in) or equivalent material must be used to line the outer framework. Side walls must be solid with sufficient ventilation as prescribed. The interior of the container must be smooth with no protrusions that the animal can bite or scratch to cause damage to the integrity of the container in any way.

The whole of one end of the container must be open, covered with bars, weldmesh or smooth expanded metal which is securely fixed to the container so that the animal cannot dislodge it.

Handling Spacer Bars/Handles

Must be provided along the middle of both long sides of the container.

Floor

The floor must be solid and leak-proof.

Roof

The roof must be solid but ventilation holes are allowed over the whole surface provided that they do not reduce the integrity of the strength of the roof itself.

Door

The door must form the whole of one end of the container. It can be either sliding or hinged.

There must be an adequate means of fastening and sealing for those containers destined for countries where sealing is required. Large doors will require additional hinges and two or three secure means of fastening to be fully secure.

The door must be constructed of plastic, welded or cast metal of sufficient gauge or thickness so as to preclude the animal from bending or distorting the door. Doors made of plastic material are permitted, provided that hinges and locking pins are made of metal of sufficient gauge and thickness.

For rigid plastic containers, the door hinge and locking pins must engage the container by at least 1.6 cm (5/8 in) beyond the horizontal extrusions above and below the door opening where the pins are fitted.

The shipper must ensure that all hardware and fasteners are in place and serviceable.

Ventilation

Ventilation is provided by an open end to the container (which can be the door) and by ventilation openings of a minimum of 2.5 cm (1 in) over the upper two thirds of the opposite end and the remaining two sides, at a distance of 10 cm (4 in) from centre to centre of each opening.

In the case of specially constructed large dog containers the open end must be covered by closely spaced metal bars or a double weld mesh with 1 cm (½ in) spacing between the meshes.

The total ventilated area must be at least 16% of the total surface of the four sides. The provision of additional holes on the roof or sides of the container or larger mesh covered holes in order to increase the ventilation are permitted.

All openings must be nose and paw-proof, in the case of cats and small dogs these may have to be covered with mesh. It is very important that no animal has any surface or edge at which it can gnaw or scratch.

Feed and Water Containers

Water container must be present within the container with outside access for filling. Food containers must be present either within the container, if sealed, or attached to it for use in cases of delay.

Forklift Spacers

Must be provided for all containers where the total weight with the animal exceeds 60 kg (132 lb).

SPF Containers

Specific Pathogen Free (SPF) dogs and cats must be transported in containers whose dimensions conform to the requirements published in this Container Requirement. SPF labelling must be affixed to the container plus "This Way Up" labels. Filter containers for SPF consignments have special gauge air filters fixed in the ventilation apertures. Ventilation must be a minimum of 16% of the surface area

of the four sides. Sufficient water must be provided for the journey. Food must be provided, if required, at the point of origin in order that the sealed container is not opened during transport. A viewing panel must be provided on SPF containers.

Labelling

A green "Live Animals" label/tag or a red "Laboratory Animals" label/tag is mandatory on all live animal consignments. "This Way Up" labels/tags are also mandatory and must be placed on all four sides of the container whenever possible. The label or tag can be imprinted on the container.

2. PREPARATIONS BEFORE DISPATCH (see Chapter 5)

Tranquillisation of dogs and cats is not recommended.

See General Container Requirements at the beginning of this chapter.

Feed the animal only a light meal and a short drink approximately two hours before dispatch and exercise the animal immediately before dispatch.

Snub nose dogs, such as boxers, bulldogs, pekinese and pugs, are affected more than other breeds by rarefied atmosphere and care must be taken to ensure that the front of the container has open bars from the top to the bottom of the box for ventilation. It is essential that the animal be free from respiratory troubles.

EXAMPLE

TYPICAL RIGID PLASTIC DOG CONTAINER

Door hinges and locking pins must extend beyond the horizontal extrusions above and below the door opening by at least 1.6 cm (⅝ in)

Spacer

Ventilation openings

Door lock

Affixed food and water container

Back view

Spacer bar

Ventilation openings

Rear of box

Food and water container with outside access

Mandatory "This Way Up" label
Mandatory (green) IATA "Live Animals" label

Notes:

1. *A maximum of two adult animals of comparable size up to 14 kg each, that are used to cohabitation, may be shipped in the same container. Animals over that weight must travel individually.*

2. *Animals up to six months old from the same litter, up to a maximum quantity of three, may be shipped in the same container/compartment.*

Shipment of females in heat (oestrus) is not recommended.

Females with suckling young and unweaned animals will not be accepted for carriage.

Weaned puppies younger than eight weeks must not be shipped due to possible dehydration effects in air transportation. Kittens likewise, younger than 8 weeks must not be shipped but it is recommended that a veterinary certificate be provided for those under 12 weeks stating the animal(s) is/are fit to be transported because of their small size, especially as some breeds, renders them more susceptible to the effects of dehydration.

Weaned puppies and kittens may travel well together. The quantity must be related to the size and strength of the individual animal. Avoid shipping a weakling which could be harmed by its companions. Certain national regulations require cats or dogs to be crated individually unless the consignment is a litter over 8 weeks with the mother.

For pet animals, a familiar article in the container helps to placate the animal. Animal's name must be marked on the outside of the container.

3. FEEDING AND WATERING GUIDE (for emergency use only)

Animals do not normally require additional feeding during 12 hours following the time of dispatch. Water must be provided if total journey time exceeds 12 hours. Care must be taken not to overfill the container.

If feeding is required due to an unforeseen delay, meat, biscuits and canned pet food must be provided but care must be taken not to overfeed.

4. GENERAL CARE AND LOADING (see Chapters 5 and 10)

Containers of young animals of the same species may be loaded adjacent to each other. Containers with cats and containers with dogs must be kept apart, unless they are used to cohabiting. Care must be taken in loading different breeds of dogs to prevent snapping and disturbing one another and, in particular, where one animal is stronger than the other, subjecting the weaker of the two to fear.

Accompanied dogs and cats that are transported in the aircraft hold must comply with these Regulations.

Warning 1: *Snub-nosed dogs must be stowed as far away as practical from other loads to ensure they have the largest amount of air space available in the hold.*

Warning 2: *If it is necessary to open the box for any reason, this must always be done in an enclosed area in order to prevent the animals from escaping.*

Animals in quarantine must be segregated from those which are not.

IATA

Recommendations for shipping your pet - dog or cat

When two or more pets travel together

The United States Department of Agriculture (USDA) Animal Welfare Act (AWA) states that "no more than two live puppies or kittens, 8 weeks to 6 months of age, that are of comparable size and weighing 20 lb. (9 kg) or less each, may be transported in the same primary enclosure via air carrier." This is a good practice to follow for all animal shipments, no matter what country they are traveling in.

Remember, animals may become stressed and aggressive when traveling by air and should not be placed in the same container unless they are young puppies or kittens. Animals which share the same household may become stressed and aggressive towards each other when traveling by air.

Some airlines restrict the maximum number of animals allowed in the cabin, check with your intended airline regarding their requirements if you are planning to carry your pet onboard.

When pets travel unaccompanied

If your pet is flying unaccompanied, the preparation of the animal is the same as when it flies with you, but you will need a Health Certificate from your veterinarian to say that the animal is healthy and fit to fly. Check the documentation requirements and regulations for your country or the importing country if the pet is traveling internationally.

Minimum container requirements, as described in the Live Animals Regulations, are mandatory for transportation of animals by air. Food and water containers (troughs) accessible from outside the container are required. The carrier, or government agency, may require that additional food be provided in a pouch attached to the container with feeding instructions.

You can either find an animal shipper who can make all the necessary reservations and take full charge from collecting your pet, boarding it if need be, taking it to the airport and have it met at the other end and delivered to destination. In some countries, this may be the easiest and surest method and some airlines will not accept animals handled by anyone other than a shipper. The airlines can usually give you a list of shippers with whom they work. But it is possible that you can do all this yourself. Check with the airline for any special requirements for shipping your pet.

Preparation for Air Transport

Before animals commence their journey, it is important that advance arrangements be made and confirmed. The most suitable routing always needs to be selected, as many airports do not have adequate facilities at destination or possible transit stops. Consideration should be given to the day on which the consignment (or consignments) is dispatched and its date of arrival, because some customs authorities and other government agencies do not work during weekends or public holidays. Advance arrangements shall include confirmation that the consignee is aware of the shipping details and has made arrangements to take delivery of the consignment on arrival.

Before the consignment is delivered to the airline, the shipper or his agent must ensure that all import and export licenses, health certificates and permits have been obtained. When these documents are required to go forward with the consignment, they must be securely attached to the air waybill. The shipper is also required to provide the airline with two correctly completed copies of the Shipper's Certification for Live Animals. It is important to note that the Shipper's Certificate also contains a declaration in relation to endangered species. An air waybill must be completed on behalf of the shipper and must clearly show the number and species of animals in the consignment. Pets accompanied by their owners do not require an air waybill and the Shipper's Certificate.

Particular care and attention should be paid when selecting the container used in the air transportation of animals, because containers must meet the minimum requirements of CR1 as published in the IATA LAR. A copy of container requirement 1 is published on the web site. Crate or container crating is very important. Purchase one in advance and get your animal used to being confined in it. Remember taking an animal out of its natural environment or surroundings is by definition stressful. You can certainly help your animal that way in coping with these new events. As a responsible pet owner, this responsibility is often overlooked.

Airlines have specific procedures in place for the acceptance, handling and delivery of your animal. The environmental needs of the animals are duly considered during loading, off-loading or at a transit stop. People loading animals should be aware of the requirements and the action to take when problems arise. Most importantly however is that the container must be able to contain the animal at all times. The Captain must always be notified of the quantity, species and location of animals onboard the aircraft.

In the best interest of animal welfare, it is essential that all aspects of the IATA Live Animals Regulations be complied with. Since many countries have incorporated the IATA Regulations into their national legislation, non-compliance may result in possible fines or confiscation of the animals or in legal action by the authorities.

Useful Websites

www.lowchensqustralia.com/quaratine

www.inspection.gc.ca

www.sailcharbonneau.com

www.dogfriendly.com

www.petsonthego.com

www.petplanet.co.uk

Travel Literature

The Basics of Boat Travel with Your Cat or Dog by Diana Jessie Seaworthy Publications, Inc. 2003 This is an informative book about traveling with pets. Diana Jessie has sailed extensively and is well-known in the cruising community. Her book focuses, primarily, on traveling with cats. She and her husband have already sailed to many of the places still on my list.

SCARY STUFF

What if we have to abandon ship?

All experienced sailors know that you never, ever, step *down* into a life raft. Your strong, well-equipped Mother Ship must be going under before you leave her for a ride in a flimsy rubber tub. However, should you need to abandon ship, you'll want to be prepared to save all the members of your crew. In my opinion, the best preparation for abandoning ship has three parts: First, a well-stocked, recently inspected life raft. Second, abandon ship practice sessions with all crew members (including your pet) participating. Finally, a carefully provisioned, easily grabbed, Ditch Bag.

The most important element of a life raft inspection, or the fitting out of a new raft, is your input. You need to make a list of what you want to go into your raft before it's sealed in its valise or hard-shell. Don't leave it up to a raft-fitting company to decide what should go in your life raft. Ask to see the items before they are packed, as quite often the standard gear is not the quality you'd want. You can start with the list provided by the raft company and then change or add to that list.

If you're purchasing your life raft new, be sure to look at the flooring. You want to have some kind of flooring that will hold up against sharp dog nails. Imagine a larger dog, trying to get a grip in a small rubber boat. Most life rafts are pretty strong but if you have any doubts about your raft's "puncture proofness," you may want to have a layer of thin indoor/outdoor carpeting placed on its floor before it's packed. I use this trick with my blow-up two person canoe. The canoe is lots of fun, packs in its own valise and can easily be strapped on top of my van. It's a great toy for playing in rivers and lakes when we're making road trips. I use the carpeting trick in the canoe to insure that Kip's nails (no matter how well clipped they might be), don't puncture the flooring. It also gives him a better grip and, I imagine, a sense of security. Because it's indoor/outdoor – designed for patios and decks – it is lightweight (I just pull it out and give it a good shake to get rid of sand). It also dries quickly and packs small enough to fit in the valise. This simple trick can save you from worrying about a possible puncture in your raft.

What goes in a Ditch Bag?

After abandoning ship and before being rescued, all your worldly possessions will be contained in your Ditch Bag. Make it as complete as possible but remember, it has to be manageable – every member of the crew should be able to lift it and get it into the raft. It should be stored in a place everyone knows about and where it can be retrieved in a split second.

You can purchase Ditch Bags of all sizes, levels of sophistication and price. The bag itself should be water resistant, and if possible, have some sort of flotation built in. In addition to empty Ditch Bags, there are several different brands of commercially filled Ditch Bags. You have a choice to either start your bag from scratch or simply add items to a pre-filled bag. By starting from scratch, you can insure the quality of each item you pack. But, of course, it's more work to make your own bag. Generally, the stocked bags run from $99 – $200. In either case, take the time to make a list of things that you and your crew would want to have if you were forced to spend several days in the raft. There are undoubtedly items specific to each member of your crew that will not be available in a commercially prepared bag.

Items Usually Found in Well Stocked Ditch Bags

<u>406 MHz EPIRB (Emergency Position Indication Radio Beacon)</u>
You'll have one on your ship but take another in your Ditch Bag. If

you can purchase one of these at a boat show, you'll probably save money, be able to find the newest model and get a lesson on how to operate this life-saving piece of equipment.

Hand and parachute flares
Make sure your flares are current and are packed in a dry bag or plastic container.

Flashlight and spare batteries
These are best packaged in separate Ziploc baggies.

Prescription medications
Be sure to include something for seasickness. I put these in Ziploc baggies as well.

Sunglasses
Enough for every member of your crew.

Eyeglasses
I ask new crew members to bring an extra pair of glasses for the Ditch Bag. Even a pair with an older prescription is better than nothing in an emergency. The same thing goes for my crew members who wear contact lenses. An extra pair and a small bottle of solution would be most welcomed in an emergency.

Long sleeved shirts, long pants and wide-brimmed hats
Again, prepare for all the members of your crew.

Heavy duty sunscreen

Waterless hand cleaner

A small fishing kit

Sharp knife
Pack this in a protective sleeve.

Small cutting board
Maybe pack some wasabi for sushi!

Handheld VHF radio and spare batteries

Mirror for signaling

Handheld compass

GPS and spare batteries

Folding bucket
Or something for bailing water.

Folded chart
At least you'll have some idea of your "route."

First aid kit
Pack with the meds not included in your raft's kit.

Notebook and pens

Watch
Set this to Greenwich Mean Time.

Small sewing kit
Be sure to include large-eyed needles and strong thread (maybe sail repair thread).

Space Blanket

Handheld water-maker or solar still

Toothbrushes and toothpaste

Toilet paper

<u>Water and food packets</u>

<u>Collapsible drinking cups</u>

<u>Chocolate bars</u>

Make sure that all your equipment has a tether or lanyard attached. It would be awful to be drifting along in your raft, watching your water-maker (just out of arm's reach) slowly sinking into the sea. Tie everything to you or to the raft.

Make photocopies of all your important papers (credit card numbers, ship's papers, passports, etc.); put these in a waterproof document holder or double bag them in Ziploc bags.

Additional Items to Add to Your Ditch Bag When Cruising with Your Dog

<u>Indoor/outdoor carpeting</u>
This might already be packed in your raft.

<u>Folding food and water bowls</u>

<u>Astro-turf</u>
If your pet is used to using a square of Astro-turf onboard, this can help her adjust to the life raft situation. You'll appreciate having a specific area to clean up as well. Of course, the idea is to be rescued quickly, not to spend an extended period of time in your raft. However, forewarned is forearmed. If you do end up in the raft for a while, you want to be as comfortable and safe as possible.

<u>Rubber gloves</u>
These are just to help you clean up, if necessary. I don't think I need to go into a lot of detail here. You get the picture.

PFD and harness

Even if your pet is a good swimmer, you'll want to take a PFD for her. Just like people, animals get exhausted in rough water and large swells. A secure harness, attached to a leash, will help you retrieve your exhausted pet if for some reason she leaves the raft. It will also assist rescuers in helping save your dog's life.

Muzzle

Remember, it may not be the U.S. Coast Guard in a shining helicopter that plucks you from peril. You may be pulled to safety by local fishermen in an ancient, leaky Chinese Junk. If you think your pet might appear threatening or might snap at your heroes, include a muzzle in your Ditch Bag.

Leash

Pack one with stainless hardware so that when you need to use it, the clasps, etc. will still function. As I mentioned, this can be used to help retrieve a dog that lands in the water. Once you reach safety, you'll probably need to keep your dog on a leash until the swirl of activities surrounding your rescue settles down.

Extra water

You want to pack enough extra water to accommodate your dog. This seems obvious but it's something that is easy to forget in the stress of prepping a life raft.

Food

Dog food can be purchased in individual foil pouches. I imagine they taste like the canine equivalent of c-rations or poorly prepared trail packets. Either way, they will keep Fido alive and healthy until help arrives.

Treats

You're going to pack chocolate for your human crew, right? How about packing a few of your dog's favorite treats? You can ration these out to help calm and reassure your buddy. He probably won't be as worried about the whole deal as your two-legged crew members, but he'll pick up on the vibes. A treat now and again can be extremely reassuring.

Copies of papers/documents
When you laminate your ship's papers along with copies of your credit cards and passports, be sure to laminate copies of your pet's health records as well. Make a photocopy of his tags and laminate it to the back of a color photograph of him. Be sure to take a copy of his tattoo or chip number and phone numbers of people to contact in case he gets separated from you.

Canine First Aid Kit
Your raft will be outfitted with a basic first aid kit (for people). If you have the opportunity to include extra items before packing, consider some of the things Fido might need. Same for the Ditch Bag. Because I give Kip meds for his arthritis, and they need to be current, I just toss a small supply of his pills in the Ditch Bag. These get rotated and replaced each trip. Check the shelf life of any other meds you might want to include. If they have a relatively short shelf life (say, one year), and you only plan to have your life raft repacked every other year, you might want to put the meds in your Ditch Bag instead.

Other medicine
According to John Vigor, author of *The Seaworthy Offshore Sailboat*, between 25 and 30 percent of all the passengers on a large passenger cruise ship will get seasick during a normal Atlantic crossing. Up to 60 percent of people adrift in life rafts will get ill. Your dog will probably get seasick if you end up bobbing around in a life raft for any amount of time. As I discussed in the section on Canine First Aid Kits, you won't want to give Fido the same meds you take for *mal de mar*. So pack some "doggy downers" in your Ditch Bag. Pack some of the medicines I described in the section on Canine First Aid Kits. Use them sparingly and keep a close eye on your dog. You want him relaxed but alert enough to be manageable when help arrives.

<u>Non-prescription remedies</u>
The essential oils in Rapid Relief®, Serene® and Flea Be Gone® are natural preservatives and have long shelf lives. You can have these products packed (unopened) in your raft or in your Ditch Bag.

The main thing to remember in all of this is that your pet is a full-on member of your crew. He needs as much attention in preparing for emergencies as any other member of the crew.

Distress Calls at Sea – Standard Format

This is the vessel _____ (repeat this 3 times).
Give your radio call sign if you have one.
Our position is _____ Latitude _____ Longitude.
Describe any landmarks (buoys, bridges, lighthouses etc.).
Describe the nature of distress (What's wrong? Are there injuries?).
Give the number of souls aboard (number of adults, number of children,
number of animals (and species).
Describe your vessel (color, power or sail, length, anything distinct).
This is the vessel _____(your boat name) standing by.

Sample Distress Call

This is the vessel Blessed Be! WDB 8480
This is the vessel Blessed Be! WDB 8480
This is the vessel Blessed Be! WDB 8480

Our position is 09° 32. 16S 138° 56. 74 W

Describe any landmarks (buoys, bridges, lighthouses, etc.)
We are approximately eight nautical miles from Hiva Oa.

Describe the nature of distress (What's wrong? Are there injuries?)
We have been dismasted. We are under engine power.
There are no injuries.

Give the number of souls aboard – number of adults – number of
children – number of animals (and species)
There are three souls aboard. Two adults and one canine.

Describe your vessel (color, power or sail, length, anything distinct)
We are a 41 foot sailboat, white hull with dark blue cockpit cover.

This is the vessel Blessed Be! WDB 8480, standing by.

What if you have to put him down and you can't reach a veterinarian?

Kitty P.Q., my blue-eyed Siamese cat, sailed the Caribbean like a brave, seasoned sailor. He rode out storms in the clothes locker, slept in patches of tropical sunlight and patrolled the decks under a canopy of glittering stars. Sometimes, he'd join us in the cockpit for an afternoon of sailing. Snuggling tight against the puppy he'd use Kip as a shield from sprays of saltwater. Celebrating with a bowl of condensed milk, he turned sixteen near the island of Guadeloupe.

After cruising for almost a full year, Kitty fell ill. A liver infection raged as he entered his ninth life. We were anchored off the island of Antigua at the time. I hitch-hiked from one end of the island to the other searching for a veterinarian – without results. Kitty's condition grew worse every day. Finally, I left the sailboat that had become home and flew LIAT (Leave Islands Any Time) Air to St. Thomas. Unfortunately, the vet care in the U.S. Virgin Islands was abysmal. Kitty continued to slide downhill. We were almost at the end of my sabbatical when I packed the shells, photos and memories I'd collected and booked a flight to Michigan. Mom and Dad could, I hoped, help me care for my ailing pet.

Snow swirled across the runway when we landed in Detroit. While "Grandpa" introduced Kip to ice-covered ponds, "Grandma" and I took Kitty to a feline specialist. The specialist ran several tests and then quietly told me he could keep Kitty alive for maybe one more month, but he'd be filled with tubes. The process would be invasive and painful. I faced the hardest decision a pet owner must ever make.

The following afternoon I prepared Kitty's burial site – a frosty patch of ground that, come Spring, would be covered with blossoms. I lined a gift box with a favorite t-shirt – one I'd worn in the Caribbean. Then, in the tradition of ancient cultures, I prepared a bundle for Kitty's journey to the next adventure. I made small bags out of paper towels and filled them with cat food. I tied the bags with brightly colored curling ribbon and then filled tissue paper packets with special cat treats. One of my grandmother's hankies cradled a tablespoon of catnip and several toy mice hid in the folds of the t-shirt. All this kept me busy as I waited, filled with deep sorrow, for the appointed hour. When it was time, Mom drove and I held Kitty on my lap. We left Kip at the house.

Mom and I didn't say anything on the ride home. Grief choked any words. Sixteen years is a long time to love a cat. Solemnly, we entered the house, prepared to put Kitty in his box, add his going-away gifts and lay him to rest in the backyard.

"Oh my word," my mother stood in the doorway staring at the sofa. Then she started to giggle. Appalled that she would be laughing at such a time, I pushed her aside. Shredded paper toweling covered the floor. Gooey clumps of tissue paper stuck like spitballs to the sofa's upholstered surface. Gutted, dead toy mice were left to bleed their stuffing on the floor. Only the catnip-filled hankie remained intact. Kip McSnip stood in the center of the destroyed burial offering, wagging his tail and grinning. He looked so cute and so happy, I had to smile, too.

We wrapped Kitty in my t-shirt and placed him, along with the catnip, in his cardboard coffin. Before closing the cover I snipped a bit of Kip's tail fur and sprinkled it over our old friend. I knew Kitty would be okay with that.

I think we are drawn to dogs because they are the uninhibited creatures
we might be if we weren't certain we knew better. They fight for honor
at the first challenge, make love with no moral restraint, and they do not
for all their marvelous instincts appear to know about death. Being such
wonderfully uncomplicated beings, they need us to do their worrying.
- George Bird Evans -

Putting a pet down is never easy, but it can be even more difficult if you're off-shore or are in a remote location without the assistance of veterinary care. We can only hope that when it's time, our little pals will go peacefully and in their sleep. Unfortunately, that's not always the case. We may be called upon to assist with their transition. As difficult a topic as this may be, it's important to think ahead and be prepared. It's part of the freedom and responsibility that comes with cruising.

So, what to do? Personally, I'd like to be able to get a prescription from my vet. Even though we've had a long-term relationship and she's treated Kip for years (and has helped us prepare for several off-shore voyages), she's uncomfortable prescribing the controlled substances necessary to put a dog down. I respect her, but I'm still left with the issue of what to do.

Fortunately, I met another boat owner who is a medical doctor. He prescribed a set of medications and gave me instructions on how to use them. I had the prescriptions filled and then printed out the instructions and put them in a separate bag in my medical kit. The prescriptions were written for me and everything I have on my boat is legal. I don't like to think about these prescriptions, but if the time comes when my dog is suffering and there is no other way to make his passing easier, I know I'll be grateful I have them onboard.

In the best of all possible worlds, we would be able to talk with our vets and our vets could share the necessary knowledge and supplies we need to assist our beloved pets with gracious and pain-free transitions. Alas, this is not the case – at least at this time. And, while I may not agree with the laws regarding what we can and cannot do, still, the law is the law. I'm not particularly interested in getting into any imperial entanglements, or asking any of my buddies in the medical profession to do so. I've told you how I've prepared, but I can't really tell you what course of action to take. However I can, legally, offer a hypothetical scenario.

You could ask a medical doctor to write a prescription for you (not for your pet). The prescription would be for Vicodin, which contains hydrocodone, an opiate. That drug is a respiratory depressant as well as a pain reliever. A large dose will cause breathing to stop. Brain function will cease after about ten to fifteen minutes of not breathing. The heart will stop once it's deprived of oxygen for five to ten minutes.

You would have to crush a whole bunch of these tablets in a small amount of warm water. The proper dosage would depend on the weight of your pet – this is something you would need to discuss with your medical doctor. To administer this liquid you would give your pet an enema, or use some sort of syringe or turkey baster to get the mixture down your pet's throat. Or, you could give your pet an injection. My doctor friend says injections are the best, and enemas are next best in terms of the absorption rate. Needles scare me (I fix serious cuts with Super Glue). And the whole enema thing doesn't work for me either. But this entire idea is simply a hypothetical scenario anyway.

Alright, you might also have, onboard, a prescription of Phenergan, an anti-nausea drug that causes sedation. It will amplify the effect of the Vicodin. You could insert four of the suppositories into your pet's rectum after giving the Vicodin. Or, you could place them between your dog's cheek and the teeth. The suppositories will dissolve and be absorbed into the blood stream.

You would have to be extremely sure that your decision was the best possible choice you could make at the time. Once you give your pet the Vicodin, you are committed. There is no turning back.

I don't know how to end this section. As I type, I glance under my desk. An 18-year old bundle of apricot fur grunts and snores. His paws twitch rhythmically. I imagine he's dreaming of swimming across a calm blue ocean with sea turtles leading the way to warmer water.

I've been carrying Kip's burial bundle (one of my old bathrobes, a few dog toys and treats) around for about four years. My friends think I'm nuts. They are probably right. But he's my best buddy and when the time comes, I want him to travel in style.

He must know I'm watching him because he wakes, yawns, stretches and then looks up at me. Those warm, brown eyes hold a look that can only mean one of two things: Either, "I love you, completely. Unconditionally," or, "Do we have any more of that cheese?"

RESOURCES

Bags

Abandon Ship Dri-Bag: This is just one of many bags on the market but it has received excellent reviews from a number of cruising magazines and authors of sailing related websites. It's waterproof (as much as any bag can be), is equipped with internal flotation and holds up to 100 lbs. of gear. Again, make sure that all crew members are capable of lifting the bag. A bag weighing 100 lbs. might be very hard for me to wrestle (in seconds) from inside the cabin to the deck to a bouncing life raft. I could do it, but it might take more time than I'd want to devote. Take a look at www.landfallnavigation.com for this item.

Rapidditch and Rapidditch Jr.: by ACR Electronics. Both bags provide built-in tether straps, external pockets for inventory lists and instant access to EPIRBs. The only major difference is the size. The Rapidditch sells for around $110 and the Rapidditch Jr. runs about $80. Both are available in West Marine outlets or online at www.westmarine.com.

Lanyards

Gear Keepers: Hammerhead Industries offers a wide selection of tools to keep your gear in place. They've designed retracting lanyards for everything from tiny pen knives to heavy flashlights. When I first looked into this company I was seeking ways to connect safety gear to my life raft. But within a couple minutes of perusing their site I was hooked or... ummm... tethered. I started finding all sorts of applications - on and off my boat - for the unique and extremely practical hardware available from this company. Check out their website; it's fun! www.gearkeepers.com

Miscellaneous supplies

For a complete selection of the items you'll need to make your own Ditch Bag, try checking out www.landfallnavigation.com. While not the best in terms of cost saving, this site does offer almost everything, including purified water packets, food ration packs, emergency fishing tackle, waterproof matches, glow sticks and mini-spear guns.

PLAY

What if my dog rolls in something on the beach?

Before you go, pack a couple of bottles of scented dog shampoo because, as you know, dogs will roll in anything. And the deader, the better. There's nothing quite as disgusting as sitting in a closed-up boat (say, during a rain storm), with the smell of decaying sealife clogging the air. Dogs who've played on the beach do smell - even after you've washed away the gooey bits.

Dog shampoo comes in four basic application forms: Liquid soap, sprays, powders and wipes. Liquid soap is the traditional shampoo in a bottle. The upside of this is that you can treat your pet for fleas and ticks at the same time you're hosing off clinging chunks of dead seal. The downside is that it requires water, and as we know, water can be a rare commodity on a boat. I've washed Kip in saltwater using plain old Hertz Mountain Flea Shampoo® and he's been squeaky clean afterwards. I've also used filtered freshwater and a sample of the most expensive shampoo available (snuck him into a fancy hotel one time - don't tell). We experienced pretty much the same results. His fur is smoother and shinier when washed in freshwater, but a saltwater bath and a quick fresh water rinse work wonders on a stinky mutt.

What kind of liquid shampoo to buy? The decision is overwhelming. There are shampoos that condition, reduce shedding (they say), lighten, and enhance natural color. You can buy shampoo that will make your dog smell like honey, cherries, oranges, the desert, the ocean, rain, almonds, oatmeal (oatmeal?) and one that helps your dog "smell natural." See what I mean? Overwhelming. Kip prefers the "Summer Peach" and I lean toward "Country Freesia." The bottom line, though, is that anything that doesn't smell like rotting rodent or festering fish is good enough for me.

If you can't use water at all, or you don't have enough space available for a proper bath, you can use the spray or powder shampoos. To use the sprays, just apply to your dog's coat with the foamy spray, rub it around a bit and then wipe it off with an old towel. Brush him once it dries. The aerosol versions of this application can get pretty pricey. You can, however, buy the product by the gallon and use a small pump bottle to apply it. Again, these come in several different fragrances - all guaranteed to be summer day fresh.

Powders work just like dry shampoo for people. They are particularly

good at absorbing grease and oil from your dog's coat. Just sprinkle the powder into your dog's fur and then brush it out. It's not quite the same as a good old soapy bath, but it's better than no cleaning at all.

You can also purchase dog cleaning wipes. They work on the same principle as a moist towelette - you just wipe your dog down and toss the product away. These work well on very small dogs or on localized areas for larger dogs. They are best for cleaning up accidents or small patches of grime.

There's one last type of shampoo you might want to consider. SNS™ makes a two-part product designed to neutralize skunk and other particularly icky odors. The first part is a spray that immediately attacks and clears the odor. The second part is a citrus scented shampoo. You can use the shampoo independently of the spray once the most offensive odors have dissipated. This system isn't cheap (about $50 for a gallon of each product, but depending on your dog's habits, it might be a good investment).

Our dog is a barker: Will this be a problem?

Actually, all dogs are "barkers." Along with tail wagging, body wriggling, snarling, howling and whining, barking is their way of communicating. Oh yes, don't forget those beautiful, baleful looks only a dog can offer – that's communication too. But for dogs, barking is just as natural as talking is for people. As you know, some people talk more than others. Just as loud talking can be annoying, continual barking can ruin a lovely evening at an otherwise peaceful anchorage. Your fellow cruisers will be grateful if you can keep your dog's barking to occasional yelps of joy or important warning messages.

Dogs bark for many different reasons. Sometimes dogs bark to get our attention. Kip isn't much of a barker, so when he does let out a yelp, I respond. Most of the time, he's telling me he needs to go out or wants more food. There are times, however, when he stands next to my desk and stares at me. If I don't stop working, he'll let out a single sharp bark jarring me into attention mode. All he really wants at these times is that I stop for a few minutes to hug and pet him. Then he'll flop back down and go to sleep again.

Dogs bark to warn us of danger, to bolster their own courage in dangerous situations and to ward off potential threats. Of course, there is the "I'm so excited! A walk! A walk! We're going for a walk!" bark as well. These last examples are not very problematic aboard a boat, though. It's the "barking just to be barking" noise that can create irritated neighbors and less-than-welcoming dockmates. While barking serves several purposes (warning, exuberance, greeting etc.), quite often it's just something for a dog to do when he's bored. Left alone a long time, Fido may begin "talking" to himself. It starts as a form of entertainment and evolves into a habit. Once the habit has developed, dogs may continue barking even though they are not alone. I'm not sure why some people don't seem to notice when their dogs (or children) are making loud, continuous noises. Maybe it's something one simply gets used to or tunes out. But let's assume, somehow, your dog has gotten into the barking habit and you want him to stop so that you - and your furry buddy - can enjoy the peace and beauty of quiet anchorages together.

It may take a while to undo a habit, but with gentle persistence you can retrain your dog to bark only when it's appropriate behavior. Here's a simple method: When your dog begins to bark (inappropriately), say "NO BARKING" very clearly while waving a treat in front of your dog's nose. When your dog stops barking to sniff the treat, keep holding the treat and tell her, "Good dog. Quiet dog. Good quiet dog." Count to three seconds (one thousand and one, one thousand and two...). If your dog is quiet the entire time, give her the treat. The next time your dog starts barking (it might be immediately), repeat the procedure but extend the counting time by one or two seconds. Remember to praise your dog for the quiet time. If your dog starts barking during the quiet time, immediately say "NO" in a sharp voice. Use the "NO BARKING" command every time your dog starts to bark - extending the quiet time and praise for a longer period each time. This may seem time consuming but dogs really do live to please us, and the reward of your affection coupled with a treat will change her behavior faster than you can imagine.

Another training method is to use the "Boogey Dog Squirt" technique – something that works especially well with younger dogs. I learned this trick when attending Puppy School with Kip. Fill a squirt gun or set a plastic spray bottle on stream mode. Put the gun/ bottle out of your dog's sight. When your dog begins to bark, give it a sharp squirt (but don't let your dog see you do it). The unpleasant blast of water in the face comes with every barking spell but doesn't appear to be coming from you. That cold water deterrent came from the "Boogie Dog." My friend has had extremely good luck training several puppies with this method. "No Bark" collars that squirt water or citronella oil at the dog's face whenever he starts barking are commercial versions of the Boogey Dog technique.

High pitched ultrasonic tones (that can only be heard by dogs) can also serve as remote trainers. The tones are triggered by your dog's bark. The sound, while unpleasant, won't hurt your dog. Devices that emit these tones are more expensive than simply working with your dog, but they work quickly, and you don't have to be present during the retraining process.

There are other methods of retraining pets, but I don't believe in using anything that hurts an animal – even if it's just a smack on the nose with a newspaper. Over Kip's entire life I've only given him a couple of smacks on his bottom (using nothing more than the flat of my hand). I honestly believe that giving your pet a great deal of constant, loving attention will yield the best possible results in terms of his behavior. As a cruiser, you'll have loads of time to spend with your dog – making this the best time to create great life-long habits!

Is it better to take two dogs cruising – so they'll have companionship?

Kip has, in fact, had furry company other than Kitty P.Q. We rescued a stray puppy on Montserrat and took care of the little fellow until we found a home for him with some other cruisers. A sleek black cat traveled with us for a while and several sea going birds

157

have hitched rides on our boat. But no other creature was quite as special as Kip's first girlfriend, Abigail O'Dwyer.

The popular cruising grounds around Washington State are busy, happy, noisy places during the summer months. But in September, when the children go back to school, they are empty. That's the time of year I take three weeks and enjoy solitary sailing on some of the most beautiful waters on the planet. The anchorages are peaceful and still. Sea creatures, now safe from hordes of picture-snapping tourists, swim by my hull, curious and interested. Kip grins and wags his tail in greeting. For many years, if we were in Washington during the Fall, it would be just Kip and me out there together. But one September evening, right before a squash-colored sun dipped into the Sound, Kip McSnip, *The Famous Sailing Dog*, fell in love.

She was an auburn-haired beauty with dark chocolate eyes. Her behavior was goofy and spacey, more befitting a blond than a redhead, but Kip didn't care. He was smitten - ears over tail, paws over whiskers, tumbling, bumbling, in love. Her name was Abigail O'Dwyer - "Abbey" to her friends.

Abbey barked in a giddy, girlish way as her owner (a fellow named Kevin), rowed his dinghy past our boat. Kip returned the greeting and ran from our stern to our bow following the slow moving Boston Whaler. Amused by their interactions, Kevin turned back and circled our boat several times. Kip ran around the deck, straining against the netting and life lines, stretching to be closer to Abbey. Abbey stood on the bow of the Whaler, leaning out as far as she could without falling in the water. It seemed the feelings were mutual.

I don't remember exactly how it went down, but Kevin and I briefly introduced ourselves and then spent the next couple of days chaperoning the two love-struck dogs. We'd motor our dinks to shore and then sit and chat like hired limo drivers while our dogs went off together. On beach runs, long-legged Abbey would slow down and wait for Kip and then, together, off they'd race. If treats were presented, Kip would stand back, letting Abbey have both hers and his. When it was time for Kevin and me to motor home to our own vessels, the dogs would pout and whine.

158

Whenever possible, Kip and Abbey were inseparable, running, swimming, barking and snuggling together. If a week went by when they were apart, they would act like lunatics, throwing themselves at

each other when they finally reconnected. Kevin and I were simply the drivers. Eventually we started saving fuel by leaving one boat at the marina when we went cruising. One weekend it occurred to me that, not counting hours at work, the four of us were spending all of our time together. I asked Kevin what we were doing – hanging around each other almost constantly?

"It's all about the dogs," he replied. "We're just here for the dogs."

We did that for almost three years. Kip and Abbey dated, Kevin and I just sort of hung out. Until one day, something changed and it wasn't possible for the chaperons to play their roles anymore. We tried to say goodbye, Kip and me, but Abbey jumped into the back seat of our car and would not come out. Kevin ended up forcefully pulling her by the collar to get her to move. Kip stayed depressed for a long time. We heard from mutual friends that Abbey got diarrhea and wouldn't eat for three days.

Kip moved on. He makes friends wherever he goes and he always seems to find at least one other dog to romp with. Tonight though, I notice him lying on deck watching the evening sky. He's lowered his head to his crossed paws. He sighs. I wonder if he's missing Abbey and if he remembers being in love.

Dogs are social creatures, pack animals by nature. When you are with your dog, you are part of the pack. Your family is the pack. Do dogs need another dog for companionship? I don't think they "need" another canine buddy - but I'm sure two dogs would always have fun together. We've met lots of cruisers who travel with two dogs. One family sails up and down the coast of Mexico with two delightful Portuguese Water Dogs. Those two look very happy standing in the bow of the dinghy. Janet and Blaine Parks, a cruising couple, sail with two large Golden Retrievers. To read about their experiences check out their absolutely delightful website www.sailcharbonneau.com.

If I had two dogs and they were part of my family, I'd find a way to take them both cruising. However, I would not get a second dog, nor would I get two puppies before I started cruising. I do not recommend getting a second dog, or getting two dogs in the first place, just so that your pet will have the companionship of another dog. For me, the issue boils down to this: It seems to me that cost, difficulties and the red tape involved in traveling with two dogs would be more than simply doubled. I'm also guessing that two dogs might limit some of the invitations to visit other boats or homes in remote villages. Again, critters who are part of my family go with me - but I would hesitate to adopt another family member while I'm still actively cruising.

Sometimes people are leery of dogs: How can we make a good first impression?

No matter where you go in the world, you will find someone who is delighted by the sight of a goofy grin and wagging tail. I don't think a single day passes without a stranger stopping his or her activity to pet Kip and to ask a question or two. It doesn't seem to matter if we're on a remote trail in a Canadian forest, a crowded beach in the south of Mexico or a bustling street in downtown Seattle. Winos and business women, toddlers and construction workers, grandmas and teenagers -

they all pause for a minute to pet Kip's fluffy head. Sometimes they ask the kinds of questions we're discussing in this book, and sometimes they tell me about one of their dogs, or even a beloved cat. Sometimes, they just chat with Kip and don't even seem to notice I'm there. That's okay with me. I figure my job is just to stand by quietly. Kip has his own job in these situations - and he's great at what he does.

Of course, it takes all kinds to make a world, and not everyone is fond of cheerful canines. Some folks are allergic to dogs and shy away from the sneezing, wheezing and rashes that come with even the slightest contact. There are also people who simply don't like dogs - or any animals for that matter. Go figure. Still others, like my mother, are afraid of dogs. Despite her good experiences with Kip, she still gives most dogs a wide berth.

Apparently, when Mom was about 12, a farm dog chased her and scared her. She was grown and married to my father when she tried to get over her fear of dogs. Dad brought a puppy home for me. I was still an infant but he thought the dog and I could grow up together. Mom tells me that the puppy, named Ivan Scavinski Scavore, never left my side. He slept under my cradle and walked close to the pram on every outing. One afternoon, for some strange reason, a member of the church next to our house put out bones soaked in poison. I guess he must have felt the need to kill the neighborhood dogs. Anyway, one of the dogs on our street brought a lethal bone into our yard while Mom, Ivan and I were getting some sun. Our little dog took a chomp on that bone and soon he began frothing. Ivan Scavinski Scavore died underneath my stroller. Mom declared that from that day forward there would be no more dogs in our house, ever again. And, except for Kip, she still harbors an aversion to dogs.

If you've been chased or threatened by a German Shepherd, it stands to reason you'd be frightened by them. If you've been hunted by dogs... well, you get the point. Unfortunately, not all people and all cultures have a positive association with dogs. So it's our job, as responsible dog owners, to take the role of insuring a sense of safety and well-being around our animals. Luckily, there are some simple things we can do to help with this task.

Unless a country is undergoing severe political unrest, most folks smile at the sight of their own nation's flag. Of course, you can't make a dog bandana from an actual flag - *that* would be asking for trouble. But you can dress your dog in a bandana sporting the colors of a country' flag. For example, in Mexico, I put a green, white and orange striped bandana on Kip. It always gets positive comments. Here, in the States, he wears a red, white and blue scarf (complete with stars). In Canada, it's something with a red and white maple leaf that gets the grins.

Recently I met a woman who rescues Pit Bulls. Because these dogs, perhaps unfairly, have been saddled with a pejorative reputation, she dresses her dogs in colorful net collars complete with stars, glitter and tiny bells. She explains that the dogs look cute and approachable in these outfits, helping people to relax long enough to get to know the dogs before making a snap judgment based on generalizations. Okay, bandanas and fru-fru may seem simple enough, but the trick works. Try it - you'll see.

What about using a muzzle?

There is a bit of a debate around the use of muzzles. I've suggested that you keep one in your Ditch Bag because rescue situations could be tense - for both your critter as well as your would-be rescuers. In that situation, a muzzle seems almost mandatory. However, when just arriving in a new environment, unless your dog needs a muzzle because of biting, nipping or other aggressive behavior, I'm not convinced using a muzzle is the best idea. Muzzles tend to look a bit frightening - they can give the impression that a dog is vicious (even if that's not the case). Try putting the muzzle on your dog and asking a couple of neutral ob-

servers what they think - first impression stuff. Then, try introducing your unmuzzled pet to a similar group of neutral observers. Gauge the reactions of both groups, then decide if using a muzzle on your dog (in a new environment) is necessary and the best decision.

Entering new territory? Leash your pet. Even if she responds well to voice commands, use a short leash or a retractable leash until you get a feel for the response of those native to the area. Keep your dog close to your side in a heel until you get a sense of how well the two of you will be received. Even if there are no leash laws where you're visiting, this is a courtesy that will win you points and welcoming smiles.

Finally and obviously (this is obvious, right?) pick up. You may be walking along what you think is just a field or a stretch of beach, but it may be someone else's yard. Respect new territories and new folks by being overly polite. You'll make it easier on yourself and your pet, and you'll help pave the way for a pleasant visit for Kip and me when we travel in your footsteps. Thank you!

Does he get along with foreign animals?

With his ready smile and fluffy tail waving, Kip McSnip gets along with everyone – people and animals alike. That's not to say, however, that he hasn't had a few out of the ordinary encounters during his lifetime of adventure. Because he's so darned friendly, Kip displays neither fear nor aggression. He simply assumes everyone else wants to sniff and play with the same open delight he shares. And, of course, that's not always the case. There have been several occasions when I've been extremely glad that Kip obeys my voice and hand commands and that he can be trusted to stay calm when necessary.

"Stop!" Captain George halted so abruptly I ran into him.

"What the – ?" I started. Captain George shushed me.

"Look," he whispered and pointed into the dark shade of the jungle forest. "Bulls." Peering around the Captain's back, I saw them. Three enormous bulls complete with rings in their giant noses and horns that would do any Texan proud. I don't know why there were bulls in a tropical forest but at the time I didn't question it. They were real, and they couldn't have been more than 15 feet away from the narrow trail we'd been hiking. I could smell their strong, musky scents.

"Don't make eye contact," Captain George said. "Keep your eyes down." Following his instructions, I lowered my eyes and noticed Kip, standing next to me, rapt with curiosity. These were something new in the animal department to be sure.

"What should we do?" I whispered.

"We're going to walk slowly and steadily right past them. And

164

don't look at them at all. We don't want to appear scared or aggressive. Don't aggravate them. Just keep moving but no running." Later, I'd question how a guy who'd been raised in Chicago, Illinois knew so much about bull psychology, but at the moment, it didn't matter.

"What about the dog?" I could feel Kip's fluffy tail brushing over my calves as it waved in greeting. New animals - a chance for new games. I could tell Kip had made a decision and was ready to trot on over and say hello to these interesting and very different sort of creatures.

"Pick him up!" Captain George hissed at me. "Don't let him bark! They could trample both of us. One gouge of a horn and your dog is dead meat."

That was enough for me. I bent down and scooped Kip into my arms. Then I spoke soft and low into his ear. "Be quiet! Good boy. Quiet boy." Kip looked up and gave me a quick lick on my chin. Captain George started walking, steadily and almost nonchalantly past the huge beasts. I followed. Kip held still, remaining quiet in my arms. Without looking, I could feel six large brown eyes following us as we passed in front of them. One of the bulls snorted, softly. And then, we were past. Moments later we were far enough away for me to set Kip down on the forest trail.

We never did figure out why those guys were there but I was, once again, extremely grateful that Kip was such a well-behaved, mindful little dog. If he'd barked, growled or ran after the bulls, I might have a very different and probably unpleasant story to tell.

Kip's willingness to please, coupled with his natural herding instinct, helped a farmer find and collect a stray calf one Spring. But his herding instinct became a bit of an issue another time when he decided to herd a group of wild goats down the slope of a hill. No matter how determined that little Border Collie was to round up those critters, the goats had different ideas. The hillside was their territory. Kip ended up exhausted and frustrated after a fruitless afternoon of attempted herding.

He's gone swimming with sea turtles in crystal clear water and has sustained long conversations – from the safe distance of our boat – with foul breathed sea lions. Seals and dolphins have performed choreographed routines for Kip's delight, and a host of seabirds have teased out many hours of joyful barking.

A couple lessons were tough. There was a donkey that wanted nothing to do with Kip and said so with a swift kick. Poor little, Kip. He limped around for several days after that encounter. He was also kicked by a horse – a blow that I thought would surely end his life. Kip survived, but he seems forever cured of the need to make friends with extremely tall, four-legged animals.

Our dear friends, Mike, Barb and their sweet little dog, Buddy, live aboard their boat in an upscale, modern marina on the central coast of Mexico. In addition to swimming pools, jewelry shops, and several restaurants, the marina hosts a small zoo stocked with exotic animals. One evening, on our way to visit our friends, Kip and I walked through the zoo. Kip gave wide berth to the zebra (too donkey-like for his tastes), was respectfully quiet at the panther's cage and barked gleefully at the parrot who could swear in three languages. But it was the monkey cage that caused a stir.

These weren't your ordinary run-of-the-mill monkeys. These guys were special – almost alien – monkeys. Some had tufts of snowy white hair, some were shaggy and others were almost bald. Their backsides were bright red and a couple of them even sported blue bums. Their tails were long and prehensile. Their faces blended nightmare grimaces with little old lady scowls. Kip stood for a long time staring at the monkeys. They seemed to taunt him with gestures, expressions and verbal assaults. They screeched at him, bared sharp teeth and shook blue bottoms in his direction. I realize I'm anthropomorphizing here, but I swear those captive primates had a thing out for Kip. It was like watching gang members in the 'hood tease a shy geek at a bus stop. Poor Kip, he looked confused and somewhat distressed – what had he done to deserve such displays of derision?

"C'mon, McSnip," I pulled on his leash. "Forget those guys. They're just weird." I tried to pull him away; we had other things to do. But Kip stayed firmly planted in front of that cage.

"Kip! Come on!" I tugged the leash again. My dog glanced at me briefly. Then he stood up and walked, purposefully, toward the monkey cage. I gave him slack on the leash and waited. Getting as close to the enclosure as was possible, Kip stood still. The monkeys went insane. Their squealing, howling, gesturing and behind-waggling behavior increased to a fevered frenzy. Then, calmly and quite deliberately, my little dog lifted his hind leg and let go - through the bars, onto the monkeys. Without a backward glance, Kip turned and trotted happily away, ready to party with his pals.

Because of his sweet personality and even temperament, Kip has been welcomed almost everywhere we've traveled. He's played babysitter for cruising children and has been invited into the homes and hearts of people world-wide. If your furry friend is calm, well-behaved and non-aggressive I can only imagine that you and your pet will be welcomed with the same warm enthusiasm offered to me and to Kip McSnip.

Which breeds make the best onboard buddies?

My standard answer for this question has always been: Take the dog you love. It seems to me that if you have a best friend, a loyal and loving companion, it's an easy decision - take your buddy on your adventure. You belong together. But what if you don't have a dog yet? What if you're planning the cruise of a lifetime or shopping for a small weekend boat and want to find a dog that will enjoy the time on the water as much as you do?

I put this question to the readers of my bi-monthly column, *Cruising with Critters*. As always, my readers – boating and animal enthusiasts

– were happy to share their stories and advice about boating with pets. Here are some of their thoughts.

One of the first things to note when you're considering getting a new pet is the size of your boat. For folks who adore smaller dogs, this isn't much of an issue. But for those who prefer larger dogs, boat size does matter. A large vessel is an advantage when you take a big dog boating. Both you and your pet will have extra room and be more comfortable in a boat with increased space. On the other hand, people who love dogs will figure out a way to snuggle even the largest of fur balls into the smallest of spaces. Probably the best authority on cruising with a "very big" dog is experienced off-shore sailor, Charlene Howard.

Charlene travels with a 110-pound Bernese Mountain Dog on her 45-foot boat, *A.J. Wanderlust*. Jackson, or "Captain Jack," has been Charlene's constant companion for all of his nine years, and she wouldn't think of leaving port without him. She can keep you laughing until your sides ache as she tells of the adventures – and misadventures – of traveling with a bear-sized pooch. Charlene offered several things to consider if you're thinking of traveling with a larger breed.

First, everything you do will be harder and more "back-breaking" with a large dog. Getting Captain Jack up and down the companionway is a continual challenge. Charlene and her traveling companion, Denny Thompson, constructed a pine plank slide which bolts over their companionway steps. This gives Captain Jack a way to get up and down from the cabin fairly easily. However, both Charlene and Denny report that the unit is more pet-than people-friendly, and they've suffered many scraped shins and bumped knees negotiating the contraption.

Another physical consideration is the difficulty of getting such a large dog back onboard after a slip into the sea. Jackson doesn't enjoy swimming, so his dips are accidents rather than play and don't happen very often. Still, when they do, the job of retrieving him is arduous. Even when using a boarding ramp and a sling, Jackson's weight – especially when he's dripping wet and wriggling – makes the job of getting him onboard a tough and sometimes dangerous challenge.

And although Charlene loves her dog dearly, she does concede that Captain Jack has, in her words, "not added to the economic value of my ship." Despite regular clipping, Jackson's nails have torn the teak decks and interior cabin soles. All of the settee fabric needs replacing, and every inch of the boat has been covered, at some point, with gooey slobber. Jackson's water dish has left a permanent stain on the flooring. Despite their best attempts to control their environment, both Denny and Charlene agree that large dogs mean extra wear and tear on a boat.

Customs rules and regulations apply equally to all animals, regardless of size, except that larger animals can, at times, be more intimidating to Customs Officials. On the other hand, Charlene tells me that almost everybody loves a big, gentle dog. Children snuggle with Jackson, adults grin, and most folks are even comfortable with a happy, slobbery slurp of his soft tongue. His greatest asset (other than being Charlene's best friend) is his ability to play the role of Ambassador Jackson. The large, smiling bundle of fur has paved the way for Denny and Charlene across four continents and twenty-four countries. He is always the first discussion point and makes friends wherever he goes.

Again, Captain Jack is Charlene's best friend and she won't travel without him for that reason. Denny, during his cruising time with them, has learned to love Jackson but offers other sailors a word of caution: "If you don't already have a dog, think carefully before making the huge commitment. Bigger dogs, like bigger boats, are more work. Decide where you want to put your energy before getting a big boat – or a big boat dog."

Okay, what about little dogs? A better bet for boaters? Well, consider Pocket, a ten year old Dandie Dinmont Terrier. He's a full time crew member on the fifty-foot charter boat, *Northwind* in Washington State. Pocket is an excellent example of a smaller dog that, despite his dislike of water, has become a well-adjusted boat buddy.

Dandie Dinmont Terriers were originally bred in Scotland and were used for routing badgers and other rodents of out dens. Pocket only weighs 28 pounds, is 18 inches high and measures 39 inches from the tip of his nose to his outstretched tail.

Pocket is the unofficial Director of Entertainment when his people, Jon and Jette Baker, take other folks out for cruises around the beautiful San Juan Islands. He is fascinated with crabbing and often "assists" in pulling crabs from their pots. He's only fallen overboard once, and unlike the difficulty of getting a heavier dog like Jackson aboard, Jon easily scooped him from the sea by simply grabbing the handle on Pocket's doggy PFD. Plus, getting him on and off the boat requires about the same effort as grabbing a small bag of groceries. And because he's so small, it's easy to give Pocket a fragrant bubble bath in the forward head when he rolls in something stinky.

Small dogs, small poops. Less food, smaller dishes, toys and other accessories. All of these are obvious advantages to a Pocket-sized pooch. On the other hand, while he can and does bark to warn off would-be intruders, Pocket will never have the deterrent value of a dog like Captain Jack.

If you search online you'll find several discussions about which breeds are "the best breeds." There are yearly survey results telling us which dogs are smartest (we *already* know Border collies are brilliant), which dogs are the best hunters, which breeds are best with children and what is the best breed of watch dog. The information is a bit daunting, so to help narrow the search I did my own "official poll" of boat dog owners and came up with the following results; they should give you a good start as you look for your own four-legged crew member.

Portuguese Water Dogs

These lovely, adaptable dogs can be found boating everywhere from Lake Michigan to the waters off the coast of Spain. They are medium-sized dogs ranging from 45 to 60 pounds. They are strong swimmers, quick learners and friendly, non-aggressive pals. Because they have short, fine hair rather than fur, they don't shed and don't smell like "wet dogs" when soaked. According to Woody and Kathy Woodside of Port Orchard, Washington, Portuguese Water Dogs make the very best four-legged crew members. Oops – there is a downside however. They do - really do - love the water, so keeping them in the boat, and dinghy, is an ongoing challenge. Kathy advises taking a stash of old towels aboard because there will always be a bunch of "drying off" time with these guys aboard.

Schipperkes (pronounced skipper-kee)

I was first introduced to this delightful breed by Neil Thompson, a Canadian sailor who has cruised with three of these intelligent, lively little dogs. Neil explained that Schipperkes were used as working dogs in the canals of Belgium. They don't like swimming but enjoy boats and very rarely get seasick. Despite their small size (around 10 to 18 pounds), they are fierce watchdogs and vigilant "vermin hunters." You'll never have a rat in the stores with one of these dogs standing watch!

While Neil thinks the world of his buddies, there are a couple of things to keep in mind if you choose a Schipperke as a traveling companion. First, they shed – a lot – and you've already read about our adventures with matted dog fur, so you know that brushing, brushing and more brushing will definitely be part of your routine with these fellows. Also, while you'll be blessed with a long term pal (this breed can live up to 20 years), they do need a great deal of exercise. Because Schipperkes are small, this isn't difficult to manage if you follow the suggestions about netting and deck walks discussed earlier.

Labrador Retrievers

Labradors have long been prized as "working water dogs." During the heyday of the Newfoundland fishing industry, Labs were used to bring nets to shore. Later they became prized hunting dogs as they will quickly jump into even the chilliest of waters to retrieve a fallen bird. Ranging from about 50 to 80 pounds they are considered large dogs. They are excellent swimmers and are easily trained (they do have limited attention spans, however, so training is best done in short, play-time sessions). They respond well to treats as rewards but Labs, like many larger dogs, are given to weight gain, so be cautious with the peanut butter. They also shed, which means we're back to the brushing activity.

Labs are sweet tempered, gentle dogs. They are friendly with almost everyone, making them less than terrific guard dogs. Still, their loud welcoming bark gives clear, advance warning whenever someone approaches. They make great family pets, and because they love to swim and get exercise through swimming they easily adapt to boating. A big down side, as with other swimmers, is that they will hop out of a dinghy and go merrily chasing after ducks, flying fish or even interesting ripples on the water. If you can learn to keep them in the dinghy you'll have a great, loving crew member.

Golden Retrievers

Like Labradors, these larger dogs are gentle, loving and easy to get along with. They are friendly to everyone and wear a non-threatening, happy smile most of the time. We told you about Kip's first and only true love, Abbey, the auburn-colored Golden Retriever. Abbey loved the water as much as Kip did, shed as much as he did, and was goofier than any animal I've ever met. Kip McSnip is a brilliant and loving dog, and he was smitten with his Golden Retriever – that should be good enough testimony for any of us!

Jack Russell Terriers

Kip and I have traveled with a rambunctious, strong-willed terrier named Romeo. Romeo, like most Jack Russells, is strong, muscular, full of energy and needs constant attention and exercise. He's smart as a whip, but left unattended for very long, he'll use his intelligence to get into mischief. This can mean digging, chewing or pulling things apart. Like his "dad" (our friend, Todd), Romeo is athletic and although he doesn't care for swimming, he loves to take long hikes and runs. This makes him an excellent companion when the two are living on shore. However, when confined for long periods to Todd's 40-foot sailboat, Romeo can be a handful. He is a fierce watchdog and can be extremely aggressive if he feels anything is out of order. Jack Russells have been known to fend off much bigger animals as well as humans. Like others of his breed, Romeo

172

is cute, vivacious and fun, but he'd probably be easiest to play with in a land-based environment with lots and lots of room.

<u>Irish Water Spaniels</u>

These majestic dogs (similar to Standard Poodles), are intelligent, bold and confident. They are generally loyal to one person, especially if they are sure that person is the established "leader of the pack." Irish Water Spaniels are strong swimmers, and their tight, curly coats make it easy for them to withstand extremely cold temperatures. While generally quiet, they will bark to warn you of intruders. Because they love the water these mid-sized dogs (40 to 65 pounds) can make good boat dogs. They do tend to drool a fair amount - something to consider if you have fabric settees. On the plus side, they don't shed or suffer from dandruff. They are mellow dogs but do need a fair amount of exercise. If you are boating in cooler climates – especially in areas where you plan to get off the boat to hike and explore – an Irish Water Spaniel might be the perfect onboard pet for you.

<u>And, and, and…</u>

Every time I query a boater about his or her dog I hear passionate opinions about how wonderful each particular breed is. "Oh yes, he sheds, but…" And, "Well, she's kind of big and heavy but still…" And, as is the case with my Canadian friend, Neil, some boaters are completely loyal to one and only one breed. So how do you really select the perfect dog for your boating experience?

Think of the size of your boat – consider how much time you'll spend on land and how much on the water. Can you exercise a dog on deck or will swimming be the main form of aerobics? How much effort will it take to retrieve a wet, wiggling critter from the sea to your deck? The size of waste material might be a factor, and just how much drool can you live with? All are important issues and considerations when selecting a new four-legged crew member. Of course, the bigger question is: Do you really want a pet onboard at all? Give these questions as much thought as you gave to the selection of your boat – your crew members are your most valuable onboard assets. Select them carefully.

I'd like to give you sage and wonderfully intelligent advice about the absolutely perfect boat dog but I don't think I can be objective. I keep remembering all the silly adventures I've shared with a dog that sheds too much, needs to run, has a thick, hot coat and is fond of herding even the strangest of foreign critters. Yes, I guess my best answer for this one is still: Take your best friend with you. Take the dog you love.

RESOURCES

Dog Shampoos
The following four examples can be purchased online at www.epetpals.com

Bio Groom Super Blue Plus: A waterless shampoo that is alcohol free. Just spray on and wipe off. The Spray Bottle is $6.50 for 8 oz. or $30 for a gallon.

Four Paws Instant Dry Shampoo: Again, a waterless shampoo. This one does not foam and has a deodorant formula. $6 for 7 oz.

Four Paws Magic Coat Dry Shampoo: This is a powder. Just shake on and brush out. $7 for 8 oz.

Nature's Miracle Pet Wipes: These "handi-wipes" pick up loose hair, dander and salt. Again, they are best used on small areas. 70 wipes for $8.

To be completely awash in choices, go to www.RyansPet.com or call 1-800-525-7387 and ask them for a catalog. If you are in a hurry, most large grocery stores have a pet supply section where you can grab a bottle of the liquid soap. For the powders, wipes, dry sprays and pet colognes you'll need to go online or visit a large chain store such as PETCO or PetSmart.

Cruising with Critters: by Jessica Stone, Ph.D. bi-monthly column on boating with pets. Boat Journal (British Columbia) and Nor'westing Magazine (U.S. Pacific Northwest).

www.stsj.com/theboat.htm This is a fun website describing Jon, Jette and Pocket!

INTO THE SUNSET

Is cruising with dogs worth it?

Well, yes. And no. You can tell from reading this book, there
are a lot of things to consider before casting the lines and sailing
into the sunset with four-legged crew. Kip and I have been doing
this for a long, long time. And I have to admit, there were places I
wanted to go that I just couldn't because dogs simply were not allowed. There have been many times when I've wanted to stay snug
and dry in my aft cabin bunk but I just couldn't. No matter how
fierce, how cold, how nasty the weather might be, a dog needing
to go out at 3:00 a.m. cannot be ignored. On the other hand, dog
walks have taken me to beautiful forests, beaches and remote trails I
would have missed on my own. With Kip, I've explored places too
dangerous to venture alone. A single woman walking the moonlit
streets of a small Mexican village might be viewed with suspicion.
But a woman walking a dog, carrying the ever-present "poop bag"
becomes part of the scenery and perfectly accepted.

Kip has been a great guard dog. Once his loud barking in the
middle of the night scared a would-be thief away from our dinghy.
Even though he's probably the most non-confrontational critter
on earth, his presence lends an air of protection around the boat.
Intruders generally avoid boats with dogs onboard.

You couldn't ask for a better watch partner than Kip McSnip
– especially in the northern latitudes. We've spent many nights sitting snuggled under a blanket together, watching Orion travel the
heavens.

Kip has been an international diplomat, paving the way for

friendly exchanges that might not have taken place without his happy, open smile. He's helped introduce me to some wonderful people. Strangers talk to people with dogs. "What kind of dog is that? How old is he? Is it a he or a she?" They tear up and tell me how much they miss a dog they knew and loved that had died. Then, embarrassed by their own candor, they wipe tears on their sleeves and bend down to give Kip McSnip one more hug. And he always returns their love with a wagging tail and a goofy doggy grin.

How much does it cost to go cruising with dogs?

I don't know how power boaters feel about this, but we sailboaters live under the delusion that when we're out there, with the engine silent and the sails unfurled, we are truly free. The truth is, there really isn't very much that's "free" about any kind of boating. Of course we have a long list of justifications about how we're actually saving money when we cruise - like, you know, "We're self-sufficient out there," and, "We're traveling in our home; we don't need hotel rooms," and, "We don't have to buy as much stuff when we live on the boat." Yep, excellent excuses; but if the truth were told, boating is expensive business. Not for a split second, however, do I feel it's *too* expensive - I'd never go *that far*! Still, there are some costs and having a dog onboard raises those a bit.

Actually, when you're on the water, there are no additional expenses. The meter starts ticking when you yell out, "Land Ho!" If you go to a place requiring quarantine time for your pet, you will have to pay for the stay. Even if you don't go ashore with your pet, some countries – Australia, for one - require that you pay for official visits from government inspectors. These can add up quickly. In several places, you are asked to post a rather substantial bond to the local government (in many places you have to post bonds for yourself and all the people aboard your vessel as well). While you generally do get bonds back, most cruisers report losing money on the deal because of exchange rates, handling "fees" and the like. And last but not least, in terms of extra expenses, there are bribes to be paid. Did I say bribes? I meant to say there are "gifts" that must be contributed to official representatives of various governments.

As I mentioned earlier, we were anchored off of Antigua when Kitty P.Q. first fell ill. To get proper care for my cat, I decided to fly to St. Thomas and then on home to Michigan, rather than cruise back to the U.S. Virgin Islands with Captain George. Foreign pets are not allowed to land on Antigua - period. That meant I had to get government permission to transport my dog and cat directly from the anchorage to the airport. The process turned out to be quite complicated.

The officials at the Port Authority were not sure of the correct procedure, so they called around and found a "vet" to assist me. It seems a relative of one of the officials just happened to be a veterinarian - or at least, that was the story. After several phone calls to the "vet," I learned that I would have to present all of my papers to him so that he could make sure they were up-to-date. No problem for me, I had everything he could possibly want, and each document was stamped and laminated. Captain George and I hitchhiked to his office, which turned out to be a falling down garage. I couldn't see anything that remotely resembled either a business or a veterinary office - unless the one, pathetically-thin dog tied to a tree was undergoing some sort of radical medical treatment not practiced in the U.S.

The man claiming to be the island's official vet wore a white shirt similar to the traditional uniform worn by most officials at small outposts. He squinted at the documents, turned them over several times and even held one up to the light. Then he told me that these were in order but that my pets were missing one shot.

"What shot?" I asked. He told me it was a shot required of all animals that fly out of Antigua. Both Captain George and I knew we were being scammed but we'd already gone through official channels and this was obviously part of the game we'd have to play.

"I don't want my animals to get the shot because it might make them sick while we are flying," I said. "Is there any other way to handle this?" The man told me I could pay $100 for each animal

- American dollars – in cash. Paid to him, of course. Otherwise, my pets would have to get "the needle." His words: "The needle." I started to argue but Captain George wisely pulled me aside and reminded me that I really had no choice and the price could go up at any time. Resigned, I made an appointment with the man to meet at the dock at 8:00 the next morning.

At the appointed hour, Captain George and I loaded Kip and Kitty into their crates and rowed the dinghy to shore. The man was waiting onshore next to his battered old car. He wanted the money up front but George had already cautioned me to keep the money until we had off-loaded at the airport. Several times along the short drive to the airport the man asked for his fee. Each time I calmly repeated that he would get his cash soon.

Once my pets were safely in line at the ticket counter, I turned to the man and, while he looked the other way, I stuffed two $100 bills in his white shirt pocket. He patted his pocket and then, without saying a word, got in his beater and left. Okay, that was several years ago, and things have probably changed. Things are undoubtedly more organized, and there are official procedures in place. But this isn't an isolated incident. Things like this happen all the time. We try to be good cruisers and avoid such exchanges, but again, forewarned is forearmed. Take some "gifts" along just in case.

What if we have to fly home with our dog?

I had hoped to continue cruising in French Polynesia after having some boat repairs done in Raiatea, but parts had to be ordered from Australia, and when the weather finally dictated that we leave the island, my boat was still not seaworthy. Stuff happens - so we made the best of it by finding a safe place for *Blessed Be!* to spend the storm season and by booking a flight home to the U.S. I hadn't planned to be flying back with Kip, so I didn't bring his regulation air crate. The only official crate available either on Raiatea or in Tahiti cost $425. That was out of the question in my mind. Using true island ingenuity, the yard owner asked his son to build a crate from heavy plywood. The young man didn't speak English and my Tahitian is pretty thin, but over morning coffee the two of us used his father's computer to go online. We found drawings of what an official crate should look like, and by late afternoon the young woodworker was proudly posing for snapshots in front of an enormous, extremely heavy - but official - wooden dog crate. I packed up everything I didn't want to leave onboard, and my dog and I were ready to go by 9:00 the next morning.

Getting Kip on the small plane in Raiatea was no problem at all. First, he was traveling in his homemade crate and everyone in the community had at least heard of, if not seen, the strange box (news travels super fast on a small island). The boatyard owner gave us a ride to the airport helping to smooth our way. His mother arrived to see us off and through goodbye tears, she draped long strings of shells around my neck. No one asked for official papers, and no one collected the extra baggage fees I'd been warned about. During the short, pleasant flight from Raiatea to Tahiti, a smiling attendant opened a passageway and let me peak at the cargo hold. Kip was safe and comfortable in an air-conditioned room filled with stacks of luggage and boxes of fresh pineapples.

When we landed in Tahiti, however, things did not go as

smoothly. I'd called the airport the day before and had gotten a set of instructions on exactly what procedures to follow. In truth, not one word of those instructions matched reality. The holding room where Kip's crate was supposed to be didn't exist. My luggage came down the chute as it should, but there were no signs of a large, homemade wooden crate. Dragging my heavy duffel bags, I went outside just in time to see Kip's box being loaded onto a cargo truck.

On foot, moving as fast as I could, I followed the truck to a warehouse. Once there, I tried to get Kip released and to figure out what we were supposed to be doing. The warehouse security people told me to go to Customs and get a release form. Then return, they told me, pick up your dog and take him back to Customs to be weighed and inspected. Leaving Kip at the warehouse, and still dragging my luggage, I headed to the other end of the airport toward Customs. Unfortunately, the uniformed Customs officials had never heard of such a thing. They sent me back to the warehouse. Along the way I rented an oversized shopping cart for the day. At least then my bags had wheels.

As far as I could tell, the official rules varied from "Absolutely no dogs allowed at all in the airport" to "Keep your pet leashed at all times" to "What dog?" Back at the warehouse, a government official waving a stack of papers fixed to a clipboard sternly told me that Kip would have to remain at the warehouse, in the crate, at all times. Our flight was scheduled to leave at 10:00 that night. There was no way I was going to leave Kip in a wooden box in a hot warehouse for 12 hours, and then put him in the same box in the belly of a huge plane for another 12 hours. I thanked the official, waited until he started harassing another confused person, and then quietly started loading Kip's crate onto the shopping cart. Yes, I know, I was definitely breaking the law.

A friendly tourist saw me struggling and stopped to help me. Now, he too, had turned criminal. With the traveler's help I pushed the cart down a ramp and away from the warehouse. The entire contraption was heavy and ungainly. The box and the rest of my bags kept shifting on the cart causing Kip to yelp in pain as he slid from one side of the crate to the other. And, it was hot. The tropical sun burned through my baseball cap and toasted the wooden crate. Finally, just out of sight of the warehouse guard station, I stopped. My clothes were soaked with sweat and my dog was suffering. I took a chance and let Kip out of the box.

Earlier, when I'd been slogging through the terminal looking for the Customs office, I had stopped to ask directions. A young college kid working as a baggage handler pointed the way. We'd chatted a moment, and when I explained what was going on he suggested I try taking my dog, and my luggage, to the Cargo Freight building at the far end of the airport.

"I think they can help you," he said.

So, with no other apparent options available, I pushed the cart and pulled my dog through the parking lot gravel toward a low brick building with CARGO FREIGHT painted across its roofline. It was my best shot.

The kid was right. We'd made it. The folks in Cargo Freight handed me a pile of documents and I dutifully wrote vital information on each one. I didn't care about the paperwork; the office was air-conditioned and they let Kip stay with me. They didn't even blink an eye when they saw him wander into the office. He snoozed at the foot of my folding chair while I filled out forms. It took about two hours of paperwork and a whole lot of money for "security fees, insurance, taxes, inspections" and other items not mentioned on the airline's website. But finally, at noon, we were free to go until 8:00 p.m. when I would have to get Kip back to the warehouse for early boarding.

"Could I leave my luggage and the crate here for the day?"

"Absolutely not," a man wearing an olive-colored suit responded. "It's policy. You are free to do what you wish but you must take everything with you." Maybe it was my obvious exhaustion or the fact that Kip was so well-behaved, but finally a woman behind one of the desks made a quiet phone call.

"Come with me," she said. Dragging, pushing and pulling all our worldly possessions, Kip and I followed her back to the warehouse. I was justifiably nervous, given our earlier "prison break." But the young woman seemed to have a plan. She led us into a small, grey office and presented us face to face with, yep, the same government official who'd told us to stay put.

My French isn't that fluid but I know flirting when I see it, and that young woman was doing some heavy-duty flirting with Mr. Government Official - on, I believe, Kip's behalf. Twenty minutes (and about sixty dollars) later we were free of the crate, free of the heavy luggage, and we had the rest of the day to explore Tahiti - or at least the airport in Tahiti.

We spent the day wandering, eating, and watching tourists. No one bothered us, no one asked to see papers, and no one admonished me about having a dog in the airport. By the time we returned to the warehouse to put Kip in his crate for the flight home, the Government Officials had left for the day. It was just security guards and baggage handlers. They petted Kip, cooed in French into his deaf ears and gently lifted his box onto a slow-moving conveyor belt headed for America.

It's probably not a good idea to break the law, and I certainly don't suggest you or anyone else do so. I'm only relating these stories to let you know how confusing the law can be. Best policy? Try to figure out what the official rules are and, of course, follow them to the letter.

You can probably tell from our story above that if you *do* have to fly your pet home it can get very expensive, very quickly. I spoke earlier about taking an official airline crate along because of the high cost of purchasing them (if it's even possible) in remote areas. Since 9/11, the security rules and regulations around bringing pets into the United States have increased tremendously. The fees have increased as well. I don't know if it's a result of politics or something else, but I have found that it's cheaper to fly your pet from Tahiti to Paris than from Tahiti to Los Angeles. The same is true for flying from Mexico to Canada versus from Mexico to the U.S. Anyone flying a pet to the States is tapped for several "security inspection" fees. My flight from Papeette to L.A. cost $925 and included wine, dinner, a movie and a full breakfast. Kip's flight, including all the fees, cost $1,250 with no meals or entertainment offered. When we landed, U.S. Customs charged us another $30, although I never did find out what that fee covered.

So let's just do a little math on some of the prices you might be expected to pay to cruise and fly home with your dog. These costs should be budgeted into your cruising kitty before you leave the dock. If you don't need to spend them, great – but it's always best to be prepared.

Some typical costs of cruising with dogs:

- Micro-chipping and onboard meds $350
- Travel crate .... $100 – $425
- Doggy PFD .... $35 – $70
- Folding Ramp $200
- Sling $160
- Local "gifts" .... $200 – $500
- Traveling dishes and other misc. stuff $175
- Airfare $1,250

Cost of sailing the seas of the world with your best, four-legged buddy?

Priceless!

CAPTAIN'S LOG

Are there treats in Heaven?

Kip is old now, almost 19. Like an old man, Kip has grown frail. He's lost his muscle tone. His legs are skinny pegs, barely strong enough to hold him up. Sometimes they don't, and he crumples, in slow motion, to the floor. His fur, once thick and fluffy - the color of honeyed apricots - is now scraggly. I can see the outline of almost every bone in his body. I pet him gently; those old bones of his are so fragile. He can't hear a thing these days, and a pale blue film covers his once-snapping brown eyes. Every morning I wipe thick goo from their corners. He looks embarrassed. I tell him not to worry; he's still a beautiful dog.

I took him to the vet the first week we were back from our recent voyage. She gave him a thorough exam and told me that except for his little body wasting away, the cataracts, the deafness and some mysterious lumps, he's in great health.

"We could biopsy the lumps," she said, almost hopeful. "Or, maybe run some blood tests?" Kip groaned and eased himself to the clinic floor.

"No thanks," I said. "We'll just wonder about the lumps."

Kip gets confused a lot these days. He stares at table legs for several minutes then growls at the offending furniture. He wanders into the closet. I guess he's looking for me. He stands there, gazing at my shoes, then lets out one, sharp bark. I go to him and slowly turn him in the opposite direction.

"Oh, there you are!" he seems to say, wagging the hairless stick that once was a fluffy feather-duster of a tail.

187

I'm not getting much sleep now – at least not much deep sleep. Kip wakes several times in the night needing to go outside. If the times were regular, like watches on a ship, my body could adjust. But there are no patterns. 1:27 a.m., 2:30, 3:00, 4:15. I'm exhausted. Sometimes I don't wake soon enough – I'm groggy with dreams and miss his call. He just can't hold things now. Again, he's embarrassed. I clean up and hug him – carefully, gently – and apologize for my part in the mistake. I tell him not to worry, he is still a really, *really* good dog.

It won't be long now. I ask, pray if you wish, that he goes on his own. Quietly, without pain. Maybe in his sleep some night during a dream of swimming with sea turtles. I think of a line in a Jerry Jeff Walker song. It's about Mr. Bojangles and how he and his dog traveled the South. Then one day, the dog, "he up and died and after 20 years Mr. Bojangles, he still grieves." I'll grieve. I'm grieving a little right now. But more than sorrow, I feel warmth. What an amazing, delightful gift this dog has given me. He's brought surprise and silliness, responsibility and great joy to my life and to my adventures.

"Will you get another dog?" My neighbor asks as she watches Kip weave unsteadily across the living room. I don't know. Not for a while. My friend Kevin says not having a dog is like having a hole in your heart. It needs to be filled. We'll see. For now, Kip and I, we're doing the best we can. I help him stand up; he teaches me about old age. Mostly, we're just hanging out together for a little bit longer. I'm doing a lot of writing – about dogs and sailing. He's doing a lot of sleeping. I like to think he's dreaming – maybe about sailing and dogs.

I am so grateful for the journey we've shared. To whomever, whatever puts puppies on earth, I whisper, *Thank You.* And yes, of course, there are *always* treats in Heaven.

APPENDIX

Life in a Mexican Barrio

We arrived at Cabo Blanco Marina in Barra de Navide on the morning of December 25th. When I opened the car door, a blast of oven-hot air hit us smack in our air-conditioned faces. Both Kip and I were eager to see our floating home again, so we ignored the heat and ran (well, hurried - old dogs don't really run much) to our boat. While Kip explored the pungent smells on Cabo Blanco's two docks, I dove into the job of putting the boat back together. Before leaving *Blessed Be!* last spring, another cruiser and I had worked for two days solid to ready her for storm season. Everything on deck had to be dismantled and stowed below. Now, of course, all that stuff had to be reassembled. And on a large old Morgan, everything is bulky and heavy. I worked, sweated and swore until it was too dark to see. Then, I collapsed.

Mexico is an incredibly noisy country. Radio music blares all day and late into the night. Church bells compete with jackhammers pounding cement; roosters herald the sun; women call to rambunctious children; men whistle; and donkeys bray. But on this Christmas night, the town of Barra de Navide was blessedly silent. I'd finally managed to clear enough space on the aft bunk to almost stretch out. I squeezed in next to the wind vane rudder and shoved a life ring to one side. Every cell in my body ached. My fingers were swollen to fat little sausages. I was too exhausted to cry.

There wasn't any electricity on the dock when I arrived and my batteries were flat. I'd given Kip the last of the potable water. The propane wouldn't light. And, and, and... maybe this wasn't such a great idea. Maybe I should have waited for a knight in shining foulies to join me. Maybe a middle-aged woman and an antique Border Collie just couldn't do this alone. I was having a Wile E. Coyote moment. You know, the one where that old Fool chases his dream/nemesis so fast he forgets to think. With smoke and dust flying behind his twirling legs, he runs right off the side of a cliff. For a second, his legs keep spinning until suddenly, they stiffen. He looks back at the cliff. Then he glances down at the million-mile drop below. In a fraction of a moment, he gets it. Gulp! Too late to turn back now. Poof! He plummets. That's me, I thought. I've run right off a cliff and I'm on my way down.

I started to snivel. And then, a little fish jumped. Imagine that, a fish, right outside my open porthole. Turning my attention to the companionway, I saw bright starlight dancing across the Christmas night sky. A soft, warm Mexican breeze fluttered through the cabin. Kip pushed his cold, wet nose against my cheek and grinned. My sniveling stopped.

One week later Kip looked up from his digging and sneezed. His nose was covered with gingerbread-colored sand. We sat on the beach watching the ocean on the first morning of the new year. Pink clouds tinged with lavender floated through pale blue morning light. I sipped strong, cinnamon-flavored coffee from a paper cup and nibbled at a chocolate-filled pastry. I was feeling pretty accomplished. After seven days of hard work, the boat looked like a real cruiser again. The aft bunk was completely clear and the dock electricity worked. We'd dinghied across the Barra Lagoon and filled jerry jugs with potable water. Old friends from the season before pointed as they recognized the fluffy yellow dog hanging over the bow of the dinghy. Then they waved to me. The night before, I'd joined a gang of cruisers, including two other

192

female single handlers, for a New Year's Eve celebration. Too beat to stay out until midnight, I'd gone back to the boat. Sitting on the foredeck, I sipped a glass of wine and with Kip snoozing at my feet, I welcomed in the New Year.

Now, I awake to the roar of large, outboard engines. Rolling over in the bunk, I close the aft hatches before strong gas fumes fill the cabin. Climbing into the cockpit, still groggy with dreams, I watch the men get ready for work. As they load their gear they call out jokes and good luck wishes. These fishermen are happy, hard-working people. Each morning they leave before dawn and return in the late afternoon to clean their catch. Their work looks extremely difficult and dangerous to me. They lift heavy fuel tanks, gut fish with razor-edged knives and head their small boats to sea in all sorts of miserable conditions. Sometimes they haul in huge billfish and marlin. Sometimes they bring kaleidoscope-colored Dorado. Sometimes, they return with nothing to clean. No blood to wash from the wooden docks.

On this morning, I watch the man with the boat next to mine make his way through pre-dawn shadows. He swaggers a bit as he holds the hand of a small boy. The child trots to keep up. I've learned that the man is Canadian, a former financial-type guy. But he left his home country years ago seeking an honest life. He married a Mexican woman. The child is his son. About halfway to the fishing skiff the man turns to the boy and hands him a heavy pole. Struggling under the weight, the boy carefully and proudly carries the pole toward his father's boat. The former business man grins, obviously pleased as he teaches his son an honorable skill.

Within ten minutes, a half dozen fishing boats have gone, leaving the marina peaceful and quiet - at least until the construction workers across the canal arrive. When they do, radios will blast, hammers will ring, and the men will whistle and call greetings across the water to me. They aren't lecherous or sexist, just neighborly and friendly-like. In the remaining moments of stillness, I watch my old dog as he snoozes peacefully on the cockpit grating. He seems to be recovering from yesterday's trauma.

It happened early, even before the arrival of the fishermen. While patrolling the deck, Kip slipped in the morning dew and fell through the center hatch. I bolted from my bunk when I heard the crashing sound and his squeal of surprise. His six-foot fall was broken by my teak writing desk, but he'd hurt his front leg when he landed. He cowered on my desk, dangling his right paw in the air, whimpering with pain. Lowering him to the floor, I consoled and quieted him while examining his leg and paw. His leg didn't appear to be broken, but I knew he'd be limping for a few days and that I'd be lifting him up and down the companionway and on and off the boat.

After several dog treats and a chunk of cheese, Kip settled down. By mid-afternoon, though, he definitely needed to go outside to do his business. Groaning, I lifted him off the boat and then followed behind as he limped toward the marina gate. His tail hung down, tucked between his legs, and he was obviously in pain. I wondered if I should look for a veterinarian.

About halfway down the dock we passed two young boys try-ing to catch minnows with handmade nets. Seeing Kip, one of the children dropped his net and tugged at my shirt.

"*Senora, esta su perro herido?*" At the time I thought the word *herido* (hurt) meant dead. My dog was wounded, but certainly not dead. I shook my head and tried to pantomime Kip's fall. The chil-dren stared at me as if, perhaps, I was *borracho* - another drunken gringo. Clearly my acting left something to be desired. Ignoring me, they turned their attention back to Kip. Serious expressions clouded their young faces as they exchanged rapid Spanish. Then, abruptly, they both dropped to their knees and threw their skinny arms around the old dog. One pushed his face into Kip's thick fur, another murmured soft words into his deaf ears. Kip's tail raised and twirled like a windmill. Then I understood: We didn't need to find a veterinarian; the Mexican boys would heal my wounded old dog with love and hugs.

It was after midnight and I was below reading. I didn't hear Kip when he decided to take a little shore leave and tour Mexico on his own. When I did realize he'd gone, I freaked. At 17 years old and completely deaf, Kip was, I figured, in no shape to be running loose. Leaving the boat open, I grabbed the ship's portable spotlight and went tearing through the darkened back alleys of the barrio dressed only in Teva® sandals, cut off pajama bottoms and a Lats and Atts Cruisier Party t-shirt. I flashed the over-powering light into doorways, down alleys and behind piles of netting. Despite Kip's deafness I kept calling his name, making quite a commotion. And I kept at it for over an hour. Heads poked from windows, young men stepped from shadows, someone whistled - sharp. I turned toward the sound.

"*Senorra, es Lassie. Lassie!*" Francisco, the night guard at Cabo Blanco, waved his arms frantically. He'd been trying to catch up

with me for about four blocks. Huffing and puffing, he gasped for breath. Francisco is a short, barrel-chested father of three. He takes his job of guarding the two-dock marina very seriously. *"Senorra - prisa* (hurry), *es Lassie!"* He pointed toward a long abandoned boat ramp at the other end of a dirt road. There were no lights and the road was dark as dirty oil. For a moment, I hesitated; then I took a deep breath and began running down the road. There, at the edge of the murky waters of the canal, dripping wet from a midnight swim and looking completely full of himself, stood my grinning Border Collie. Tears of relief mixed with the dust and dirt kicked up from the road. I must have looked frightening as I emerged from the darkness, dragging Kip by the collar. I hugged Francisco, thanked him repeatedly and called him my hero, my *Protectorate.*

The story of the crazy gringo girl running around in the middle of the night calling for a deaf *perro* spread quickly though the barrio. Local residents, the fishermen and of course, the guys on the construction site all heard the tale. Kip became a star - the little *Macho Lassie.* Me, I was pretty much the fool. No matter where we walked after that, someone would stop us, pet Kip then waggle a finger at me and admonish me to keep the leash on my aging friend. Francisco proudly retold the story with increasing emphasis on his heroic role. From that night on, Francisco introduced himself as the *Protectorate of Yesica.*

We'll be leaving Barra de Navidad soon. It's time. I've grown to love this little town with her glistening fishing nets, her gypsies selling hand-beaded jewelry and her old women sweeping the dirt away from the front of their homes. I'll miss her ringing church bells and her choir of roosters. But it's time - time to move. Spend too long in one spot and you forget how to sail. You forget about the roll of the sea and the wind. And you forget how to take a chance. It's important to remember these things. And so, very soon, I'll watch for high tide and slip the dock lines. When I pull out, I know the construction workers across the canal will stop their hammering for a few minutes and watch. Then, they'll smile and whistle - all neighborly and friendly-like.

Reprinted with permission from <u>Latitudes and Attitudes Magazine</u>, FTW Publishing, Redondo Beach, CA. Vols. 1 and 6, 2006

ACKNOWLEDGMENTS

As all skippers know, it takes many helping hands to launch a ship. The same is true for writing a book. While Kip McSnip and I take full responsibility for the contents of *Doggy on Deck*, we couldn't have sailed this course without a great deal of help from our friends.

I'd like to say thanks to Daddy who slipped me a hundred dollars when I first decided to get a dog. He understood that there's really no such thing as a "free puppy." And thanks also to my mom, who battled her fear of canines to become the best "grandma" a dog could ever have. George Getman keeps us out of legal storms and Auntie Elizabeth Bloom offers her heart and home when we return, weary and worn, from our travels.

I appreciate my colleagues at the University of Washington, School of Business Administration. Some of them are sailors, all of them are scholars. They understand the need for exploration and growth. I'm grateful to Bruce Rogers at Murphy's Landing who manages my slip and reminds me to live life right now. My dear friend, Nancy Ging, is my web wizard.

Allison Gross and Bliss Cochran are the editors writers dream about. James Shipley of Walking Cat Design is amazing. Just glance at the cover and layout of this book to see his brand of genius. Heather Owens, a first-year art student, worked hard on the original illustrations. Thanks to the folks at Sip 'n' Ship, in Ballard, for letting me Bogart a table for months while I wrote this book. Thanks also to Stephanie Hamilton for her cute photos of the dressed-up Pit Bulls.

Special thanks to the sea captains who've encouraged, chastised, berated and befriended us — each one of them pushing me (and therefore, Kip) into taking whatever risks were required. Captain George and Betty Pierce spring to mind. David Walker of Wahoo Adventures and Denny Thompson of Discovery Sailing are high on the list. And there was one old sailor, sitting on a sinking dock in a ratty marina somewhere, who told me to buy a Morgan Out Island. Many thanks to you, Captain – wherever you are.

I'm thankful to the crew members who've taught me more than they realized. While too numerous to name here, each one is too important to ever forget. Mike Irvine and I have traveled far, and well, together. I expect we have a few more oceans to cross.

Elizabeth Engstrom and Elizabeth George are cherished mentors; they are beautiful, inspirational women who are more than famous writers – they are dog lovers.

The sea sets us adrift and then brings us together again – if only for a short while. There have been people of different colors and cultures who've shared moments of laughter over some silly dog trick. Customs officials, government inspectors, policemen and members of several Navies have added to our adventures. Island people, children and fishermen have become extended family.

The cruising community is also an extended family. I appreciate those who stay on the docks, tending the lines when the storms come - they make it safe to return. I delight in those who take the jump, risking sanity and sameness, to untie and go. Sailors like Tania Abbie and Bob Bitchin have helped us learn the ropes. Kevin O'Dwyer and Abbey will forever be part of our story, as will Todd and Romeo. Michael Daily, with Samson and Delilah, are still here with us. Oh yeah, and there's Captain Woody. He's always around, with the right words, when I really need him.

I appreciate all the people who dedicate their hearts and re-sources to caring for animals. Most of all, I am grateful to Kip McSnip, the fluffy yellow dog who made this voyage such a grand adventure. He is unconditional love in an apricot-colored coat.

ABOUT THE AUTHORS

Kip McSnip,
The Famous Sailing Dog

Kip McSnip, *The Famous Sailing Dog*, went sailboarding in St. Thomas, flew in a float plane over Puget Sound and rode a motorcycle in Mexico. He's gone swimming with sea turtles and herded wild goats across a tropical island. Kip McSnip celebrated his 18th birthday while crossing the Equator in March 2006.

Jessica H. Stone, Ph.D.

Dr. Stone is an author, educator and avid sailor. She is a ghost-writer with a library of work under her pen. Jessica specializes in writing personal biographies and stories in the style of the Great American Novel. She spends her time in the Pacific Northwest and aboard her 41' sailboat, *Blessed Be!*, in the tropics.

Two Invitations for You!

Share Your Story

The publisher of *Doggy on Deck* would like to invite YOU to share your sea stories. Tell us about your boating adventures (whether you share the adventure with critters or not). Send your stories to penchantpress@gmail.com. Be sure to include a sentence giving us your contact information and permission to use your story in future publications.

Hear About Cruising Adventures Firsthand

Dr. Jessica Stone has extensive experience cruising with Kip McSnip and with a wide variety of two-legged crew members as well. She was dismasted while crossing the South Pacific and watched as a boatyard in French Polynesia dropped her sailboat's engine from eight feet in the air. Undaunted, she patched things together and kept cruising.

Jessica Stone offers lively, upbeat and informative presentations on cruising with dogs, on getting (and getting rid of) crew members and surviving less-than-perfect adventures at sea. Dr. Stone is a sought-after speaker and enjoys sharing her stories with audiences at boat shows, yacht clubs, public service organizations (such as Rotary and the Lions), and groups like the U.S. Coast Guard and chapters of the U.S. Power Squadron. To schedule Dr. Stone for your organization contact us at penchantpress@gmail.com.

Happy Boating!
Penchant Press International

What They're Barking About...

"Entertaining and Encyclopedic!"
Nor' Westing: The Family Boating Magazine

"As I read this book with my dog curled up at my side, I laughed, wept and laughed again...

...Whether you have a dog or a boat or even if you don't – this book will entertain you with the doggy antics lovingly recalled by the author who, like many of us, has embraced a four-legged creature as a full-fledged member of the family."
Dorthy Dubia "The Book Locker" Boat Journal

"As complete a guide as you will ever find - it answers every question you can think of and puts your fears to rest. And besides all that, it's good, interesting reading for any dog lover!"
Sue Morgan – Editor of Latitudes and Attitudes Magazine

"This is an absolute must-read book for dog lovers and boaters – it's the best we've ever seen. Sure wish we'd had this book when we were boating with our dogs (and with our teenagers!)."
Jo Bailey & Carl Nyberg,
co-authors of Gunkholing in the San Juan Islands.

"This book is an excellent source of practical suggestions for anyone traveling with a dog on land or sea. Jessica's extensive cruising with her dog shows how traveling with a pet gives an owner additional responsibilities that are amply rewarded with companionship and devotion."
Margo Wood, author of Charlie's Charts – World Cruising Guides